Circa 1970. A casual moment.

DAVID BOWIE
PROFILE

CHRIS CHARLESWORTH spent six years as a staff
writer on the Melody Maker, the final three as
their US Editor based in New York. In 1979/80 he was
employed by RCA Records handling publicity
for David Bowie and others. He has also contributed
articles to Creem, Circus, Smash Hits, the
Soho Weekly News, Record Mirror and Record Business.

Author's Acknowledgements

FEW PERFORMERS in rock have enjoyed as much publicity as David Bowie, which makes the task of the biographer a good deal easier than with other artists. Of necessity, unauthorized biographies rely on research work and the author wishes to thank Ray Coleman of the *Melody Maker* for allowing unrestricted access to the magazine's extensive files and xerox machine. The following books and publications have also provided material for this biography: *The David Bowie Story* by George Tremlett; *David Robert Jones Bowie, the Discography of a Generalist, 1962-1979* by David Jeffrey Fletcher; *David Bowie, an Illustrated Discography* by Stuart Hoggard; the *New Musical Express*; *Rolling Stone*. Thanks are also due to what remains of the press office at RCA Records, Fiona for memories of Mainman and Jennifer for correcting reams of shabby typing.

Picture Acknowledgements

The compilers would like to pay acknowledgement to the following organizations, journals and individuals for the use of photographic material reproduced in this book: Decca Records (UK) Ltd., E.M.I. Records, R.C.A. Ltd., Mainman, Sunday Times Colour Magazine, Melody Maker, Record Mirror, New Musical Express, Sounds, The Sunday People, Creem, Daily Mirror, Rock Scene, The Sun, Trouser Press, Grooves, Nick Latzoni Collection, Ron Newman, Lee Childers, David Jeffrey Fletcher, Bob Massineo, Andy Kent, Peter Stone, Tony Prime, Paul Cox, Barry Plummer, Peter Till, Vincent McEvoy, Henry Daniels, Mick Rock, Neil Preston, Jerry Aronson, H. Aoyagi, Scott Weiner, Ron Galella and John Mottershead. Every attempt has been made to contact the copyright proprietors, where known, for permission to include their work. However in some instances, despite repeated attempts, contact has not been possible.

Cover (Front): *Fall 1979. The "Lodger" in New York.*

Cover (Back): *Bowie performing as The Thin White Duke on his 1976 World Tour.*

Title Page: *February 25, 1981, The New London Theatre. Bowie receives Best Male Singer Award in the 1980 Rock and Pop Awards sponsored by the Daily Mirror and the BBC. All winners are voted for by the buying public.*

PROTEUS BOOKS is an imprint of The Proteus Publishing Group.

United States
PROTEUS PUBLISHING CO., INC.
733 Third Avenue
New York, N.Y. 10017.
Distributed by:
THE SCRIBNER BOOK COMPANIES, INC.
597 Fifth Avenue
New York, N.Y. 10017.

United Kingdom
PROTEUS (PUBLISHING) LIMITED,
Bremar House,
Sale Place,
London, W2 1PT.

ISBN 0 906071 67 4 (p/b)
ISBN 0 906071 82 8 (h/b)

First published in 1981.

Printed by Jolly & Barber Ltd., Rugby.
Bound by William Brendon & Son, Tiptree, Essex.
Design & Artwork by Classic Publications, Manchester.

DAVID BOWIE
PROFILE

by Chris Charlesworth

A SAVOY EDITIONS BOOK

INTRODUCTION

Early days in Brixton.

WHEN DAVID BOWIE stepped on to the Broadway stage last autumn to portray Elephant Man John Merrick, it was the climax to a decade which has seen this chameleon of the arts emerge as the most significant performer that British rock has produced.

David Bowie was born on Elvis Presley's birthday, but in 1947 there was no rock'n'roll, no top thirty and the solid bodied electric guitar was only a gleam in Leo Fender's eye. Sheet music outsold records, and the hits of the day (as heard on the BBC Light Programme) were reproduced at home on brittle 12 inch 78 rpm records or, more often than not, on the family piano.

As Bowie came of age, so did the record industry. By the time David was at secondary school vinyl 45s had replaced 78s and the 33⅓ rpm stereo long-player was striding into the market place. Elvis Presley launched rock'n'roll into a million households and seven years later the Beatles loosened America's stranglehold on popular music, capturing the public imagination and influencing scores of youngsters to whom rock was a life-line to paradise.

One of them, undoubtedly, was David Bowie. Although — as we shall see later — the musically creative sixties brought a series of personal failures for Bowie, the seventies offered a perfect platform for his uncompromising style. At a time when the record industry enjoyed huge commercial returns, David Bowie became a star of colossal proportions, the archetype glam-rocker who in turn influenced another generation of musically inclined youngsters.

But David Bowie was different from his peers. As the adulation grew, he became increasingly uncomfortable in his role as a rock star, although his contribution to the medium placed him in a unique category. Unlike other performers in rock, who operated within its limits, Bowie consistently stretched those boundaries, refusing to tread water and reap the commercial rewards of repeating a proven formula. In so doing he invented glitter rock, took rock theater to its ultimate limits, presaged the disco boom of the mid-seventies and spearheaded the stark electronic new wave renaissance.

These accomplishments, by and large, have ensured that Bowie has maintained an artistic credibility enjoyed by few of his peers. While a host of rock stars emerged during Bowie's first flowering, almost all of them have faded into an early retirement or chosen to perpetuate their careers by constantly reproducing the music of their prime period. The aging star, trading on past glories, is a sight all too familiar in the current theater of rock, but Bowie's artistic integrity and penchant for change and experiment keeps him far apart from such inelegant and undignified posturing.

So it was that when the rock star moniker became an overweight burden Bowie turned his talents to other outlets and donned a cloak of anonymity inspired by his sojourn in Berlin, the very antithesis of all that Hollywood represents. He became an accomplished actor, first on film and then on stage, and re-discovered his interest in fine arts. Simultaneously Bowie produced music that stayed one step ahead of his contemporaries yet was still accessible to public taste. The summer of the new decade saw a Bowie single at number one in the charts, a position he most certainly hadn't sought but which proved his ability to communicate to the new generation of rock fans.

Anyone who has followed the rock scene closely for any length of time, though, knows that talent alone is not enough to turn a musician into a star. Personality, imagination, timing, marketing, luck and, unfortunately, a smattering of hype, are all ingredients of the same pot-pourri that launched David Bowie.

As a manipulator of the media, Bowie has few equals: his many disguises and often vacillating opinions have constantly intrigued the serious and music press, while his one-time sexual ambiguity is still a hook for the tabloids. The fact that David's personal life is now — and has been for the past five years — a very private concern, makes no difference. Lurid tales of bisexuality are still dished up from time to time despite the fact that this kind of publicity, stemming from the Ziggy Stardust era, is both unwelcome and irrelevant. Nevertheless the skeleton refuses to lie down.

The rock scene is littered with the corpses of just as many talented artists who were unable to project themselves, as it is with untalented buffoons who flashed in the proverbial pan. Given the right circumstances, talent will always sustain an orbiting star, the quality and quantity of that talent being in direct proportion to the length of stardom enjoyed by the individual artist.

'Overnight successes' are, more often than not, 'one hit wonders', while the genuinely talented artist who struggles through long periods of hardship is inevitably the one whose ultimate accolade is artistically justified.

This truism is essential to an understanding of David Bowie's career. The narrative that follows chronicles the story of an artist struggling not only with periods of indifference but against the manipulations of a pop process that, he realized albeit too late, were foreign to his nature — and, more importantly, to the nature of his art.

1965. Davy Jones and the Lower Third.

1964. David Bowie's first single.

ONE

Mid-1960s. The Mod Look.

DAVID BOWIE was born David Robert Jones on January 8, 1947, at 40 Stansfield Road, Brixton, in South London. His parents, Hayward Stanton Jones and Margaret Mary Burns, were unmarried at the time because Hayward was waiting for a divorce from his first wife, Hilda Sullivan. He already had a daughter, Annette, from this marriage, while Margaret Burns had a seven-year-old son, Terry. Hayward and Margaret were married on September 12 the same year — a month after Hayward's divorce became absolute. They had no further children.

David's Yorkshire-born father had at one time managed a London club which ran into financial difficulties, but by the time David was born he had settled down as a public relations officer for Doctor Barnardo's Homes, the charity for orphans. He was later to be appointed the Chief Appeals Administrator for Doctor Barnardo's.

Though Brixton is a poor neighborhood, Margaret and Hayward Jones provided David with a good home. Unlike other children from these streets which surround Brixton Prison, David was never hungry when he left for school and his creative instincts were always encouraged. At the age of eight David (and his step-brother) spent two years in Yorkshire, staying at an uncle's farmhouse near Doncaster. In 1955 the two boys returned south to live with their parents at 4, Plaistow Grove, Bromley, a suburban town in Kent. There David attended Bromley Technical High School.

David's first musical influence was Terry, an avid jazz fan who listened to John Coltrane, read books by American 'beat' writers Kerouac, Kesey and Ginsberg and haunted London's jazz cellars by night. Filled with wanderlust, Terry left home to join the Merchant Navy while David was still at school, but he seems to have been an important early influence. Either way, David's purchase of a saxophone at the age of twelve was a direct link with Terry Jones.

At that time trad jazz — a watery distillation of the New Orleans syncopated ragtime style — was enjoying a brief popularity in England. The urgency of the first wave of classic American rock and rollers had given way to a period of listless dormancy on the British pop scene: Elvis, fresh from the Army, was no longer a rebel, Cliff and the Shadows were becoming too wholesome and crooners like Frank Ifield were dominating the charts.

So David turned to jazz, but he also discovered King Curtis whose rasping tenor added the inimitable honk to so many early rock and roll records. He took lessons on the saxophone and, by the age of 15, was playing with a school group, George and The Dragons, whose only recorded appearance was at the High School Christmas Pageant in 1962. They shared the billing, incidentally, with a younger group called The Little Ravens whose guitarist was Peter Frampton. Frampton's father, a master at the school, arranged the affair but by all accounts it was David who stole the show, soloing on the saxophone with all the exaggerated cool that jazz improvization inspires.

It was shortly after this affair that David's eye was injured in a scrap with schoolfriend/fellow musician George Underwood. Hostilities erupted over George's girlfriend and David wound up in hospital for two months while doctors unsuccessfully attempted to restore his pupillary muscles. To this day the muscles have been paralyzed, giving David a curious, but not unattractive, facial quirk. One eye is blue and the other grey, with one pupil considerably larger than the other.

In 1963 David left school with 'O' levels in Art and Woodwork. For six months he worked as a commercial artist, an experience he did not relish and which he glossed over in later interviews. "I hated it," he was to say later. "For six months I tripped out on capitalism." In the evenings David continued to play his saxophone with a jazz group in Bromley.

That same year the torpid British music scene received the jolt that scores of young musicians were anticipating: the beat boom. Led by the Beatles, groups from Merseyside and beyond descended on London in droves, making records that scorched up the charts and injecting a shot of adrenalin into the music industry that opened the doors for a whole new breed of young performers. The reverberations of the shock linger to this day as the Beatles and their imitators brought a completely new sound to the pop scene, a raw, refreshing blend of electric guitars, drums and vocal harmony that sent out a message of pure optimism to Britain's frustrated youth. The rock race was on and David Jones was one of hundreds of unseeded starters.

David's reaction was to switch from jazz to pop and form a new group, the King Bees, with "some guys from Brixton I met in a barber's shop". The line-up was Bob Allen, Dick Underwood, Frank Howard and Roger Bluck, and the group concentrated on rhythm and blues. For six months the King Bees worked the local circuit, but in early 1964 David took it on himself to write to washing machine magnate John Bloom seeking finance for the group.

The choice of John

1961. Royston Ellis's book is the first serious book treatment of rock music to appear in the U.K. The leading British Beat/Rock writer, Ellis proves to be very influential to most rock performers up until 1966.

Bloom for a potential sponsor was not quite so absurd as it may sound. Bloom's escalating fortune was a passport to the pop scene, and he was known to throw lavish parties for musicians and entertainers before his Rolls-Razor

Nik Cohn's "Johnny Angelo" is the best rock'n'roll novel ever written, and David Bowie's favorite rock book! Ziggy Stardust is to be partially modeled on the book's central character.

1965. David Bowie's third and fourth singles (and their B-sides) released as an EP from E.M.I. in August.

1966. David the Mod pours himself a large vodka.

Jane which Decca released on their Vocalion label in June, 1964. The 'B' side was a cover of a Paul Revere and the Raiders number entitled *Louie, Louie Go Home*. After it flopped Decca released a follow-up, *You're Holding Me Down*, a month later on their Coral label. This suffered a similar fate, Decca lost interest and it was only a matter of time before the dejected King Bees called it a day.

The net result of this experience was not all

business empire collapsed. Bloom actually replied to David's letter, suggesting that he contact a friend, impresario Les Conn, who in turn persuaded Decca Records to record the group. The old established British record company had just made up for rejecting the Beatles by signing the

Rolling Stones and they saw no reason why another R' and 'B group shouldn't emulate the success of Jagger and Co. It was, alas, wishful thinking on the part of Decca.

Thus David's first appearance on vinyl was a song written and produced by Les Conn called *Liza*

Summer 1965. Official photograph.

negative. Through Decca, David met his first manager, Ralph Horton, a former roadie with the Moody Blues who in turn introduced David to Ken Pitt, the professional manager who was to handle David's career for the next five years. Undoubtedly it was Horton who inadvertently put David Jones on the ladder to success.

The year is 1965 and the London music scene is a seething pit of managerial

sharks all anxious to make a quick profit in the rapidly expanding pop industry. The extraordinary success of the Beatles and their peers has attracted a new type of hustler to the music scene and these sharp, unrepentant visionaries congregate in the bars and clubs that surround Soho's Wardour Street, the mecca of the British movie and music industries. Deals are made, contracts are hastily signed and careers are bartered over large vodkas at The Ship, De Hems or La Chasse, the one-room private club above the Marquee. Eighteen-year-old David Jones, already shown the door by one record company, is indeed fortunate to have fallen in with an honest and experienced manager so early in his career.

His next band, before Pitt's arrival, was the Mannish Boys — in fact for a short period, until the King Bees folded, he was a member of two groups at the same time. With the MB's David supported a number of popular artists of the day, including Gene Pitney, the Kinks, and Gerry and the Pacemakers, and recorded two singles for EMI's Parlophone label.

The first, *Take My Tip*, was credited to David Jones and the Mannish Boys and the second, *You've Got A Habit Of Leaving*, just to David Jones. Both were released in the summer of 1965 by which time David had actually abandoned the group and was calling himself Davy; hoping, apparently, to conjure up

Kenneth Pitt — David Bowie's first real manager.

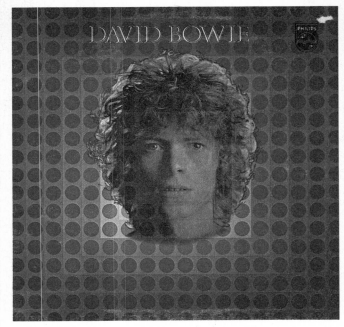

Top Left: *Circa 1969. Bowie around the time he recorded "Space Oddity".*
Top Right: *1971. The Man Who Sold the World. Wearing his Mr. Fish "man's dress" on the notorious album sleeve.* **Bottom Left:** *1971. The cosmic rocker recently arrived — Ziggy in gestation.* **Bottom Centre:** *1972. Ziggy onstage playing 12-string guitar, with Trevor Bolder in background.*

David Bowie: A Profile 9

DAVID BOWIE AND THE BUZZ

FRIDAY 15th JULY
7. 30 - 10. 30pm.
Members & Guests
4/-   5/-

LOUGHTON YOUTH CENTRE

1966/67? Ticket for an early concert.

138

Film still from the unreleased "Love You Till Tuesday" financed by Ken Pitt to promote the album of the same name (album released June 1967). The film portrays David Bowie as Major Tom, singing his first-ever hit — "Space Oddity".

visions of nautical endeavor.

Both records sank without trace but Horton managed to book David into various West End clubs including the Marquee, perhaps the best known and certainly the longest running rock club in town. The Marquee booking — at which David backed the High Numbers, soon to become the Who — led to an invitation to tape six shows for broadcasting on Radio London, the pirate radio station.

In the mid-sixties pirate radio stations, which pumped out non-stop pop, played a colorful and important part in the promotion of records. These offshore stations were both illegal and irreverent but their format was light years ahead of the staid BBC Light Programme. With the simultaneous spread of pocket sized transistor radios, the pirates ruled the airwaves and it took the Government to eventually sink them. Nevertheless the pirates led directly to the formation of Radio One and its pure pop format. The BBC even hired most

of the early Radio One DJ's from the pirate ships.

For the Marquee broadcasts David formed a new group, The Lower Third, comprising Dennis Taylor on guitar, Graham Rivens on bass and Phil Lancaster on drums. The sessions took place on Sunday afternoons, and Ralph Horton, realizing that he needed some help in managing David, invited Ken Pitt to one of the shows. Pitt was impressed.

"I was looking for someone who could come out of the pop world and be a star as opposed to a guitar cowboy," said Pitt later. "When I saw David for the first time down at the Marquee, I thought he was someone who could be groomed in the way I had in mind."

What Pitt had in mind was an all-round entertainer, a singer who could dance, a dancer who could tell jokes, and a comedian who wrote songs and played guitar. It was, of course, an old-fashioned image, a far cry from what David was to become, but Pitt's long-term ambitions for David were founded on show business principles and he was, essentially, a

Circa 1968. Official photograph.

traditional show business manager. More to the point, he was honest and he meant well — and he was impressed with the songs that David performed.

One of the first things that Pitt did was to advise David to change his name. On a recent trip to America he had seen the Monkees TV show which featured another Davy Jones as lead singer of the group. Thus David Jones of Bromley became David Bowie. He selected the name himself, apparently taken from the Bowie knife so popular in Western movies.

A meeting between David, Horton and Pitt resulted in a new record deal — this time with Pye Records who appointed their star producer, Tony Hatch, as David's Recording Manager. The first David Bowie single *Can't Help Thinking About Me*, a song David had performed during the Marquee sessions, was released by Pye on January 14, 1966, and an accompanying press release Jones Is Back In His Locker." It went on to describe David's talents in the mixture of exaggeration and superlatives common to such documents to this day.

In April Ken Pitt officially took over David's management after consultation with his parents. David's father, in particular, was anxious that his son should have expert guidance and he formed a close relationship with Pitt over the next three years. Mr Jones had been aware for some time that he had

bred an unusual son, but he was determined not to stand in the way of David's artistic ambition. David himself moved into the spare room of Ken Pitt's flat in Manchester Square, just off Oxford Street.

By this time David Bowie and the Lower Third had embarked on the time-honored group tradition of traveling up and down the country on an endless series of one-night stands. They traveled, for a while, in an old ambulance which was fitted out with rudimentary sleeping accommodation to save money on hotel bills. But David's life was a good deal more comfortable than that of the average gigging musician. "In London he stayed with his parents or me," said Pitt. "He knew he always had a nice house to go back to. He was never broke in the sense that so many other musicians have been. He was never destitute, never on the streets with nowhere to sleep with no food and no money in his pocket."

Pye followed up *Can't Help Thinking About Me* four months later with *Do Anything You Say*, another original composition by David. In August they released their third and final single *I Dig Everything* which, like the others, was produced by Tony Hatch. None of the Pye records clicked and, since Hatch and Bowie didn't see eye to eye, he was released from his contract.

"David was the first real singer/songwriter and was very stimulating in the studio, but I knew he

would not have a hit with me because he was not ready," said Hatch later. "For every great artist there is a time when they happen, and that time hadn't come yet."

Discouraged by the dismal response to his records, David sacked the Lower Third and concentrated on a solo career, performing at the Marquee on Sunday afternoon sessions before a growing audience of disciples that usually included his mother. He also extended his sphere of operations — with Pitt's assistance and encouragement — to include film work, television and modeling. The money from these projects sustained David until December when Pitt managed to pull off another record deal, this time with Deram, an independent label started by producer Denny Cordell, and distributed through his old friends, Decca.

Four record labels in two years seems like an extraordinary track record by today's standards and, indeed, David was fortunate to be able to continue recording after so many flops. The mechanics of the pop industry are such that record companies can enter into 'single-only' deals whereby they are entitled to drop the artist if some degree of success is not attained after three, or even two, releases. Such deals still occur today, but they were far more common in the sixties before the concept of artist development was recognized. Inevitably

Circa 1967/68. Reclining on bed.

Circa 1968/9. With young admirer and minus hair for bit part role in "Virgin Soldiers".

Circa 1968/69. With perm, following visit to hairdressers.

advances were minimal, barely enough to cover recording costs, and, should a single succeed, the artist found himself bound to the record company for a lengthy period.

With David leaning towards a mod image, Deram issued *Rubber Band* backed up with *London Boys*, a mistake since the flipside was both superior and more topical, but the company chose to promote their only other artist at the time, Cat Stevens, who was meeting with substantially more success in the record stores. The follow-up, *Laughing Gnome*, released in April, 1967, sounded remarkably like Tony Newley who, along with Bob Dylan, seemed to be David's main musical influence.

Outside of the studio, though, other influences were making themselves felt. The year 1967 saw David flirting with a variety of images and interests, realizing, perhaps for the first time, that there was more to his creative ambition than simply being a successful pop star. It was a dilemma that David would face throughout his life.

Firstly there was Buddhism, a doctrine that had interested David over the previous year and which he mentioned in an interview with Chris Welch of the *Melody Maker*, one of the first rock writers to take an interest in David's career. "As far as I'm concerned the whole idea of Western life is wrong," he told Welch. "I write my songs about the people who live in London and the lack of real life they have. The majority just don't know what life is."

David's interest in Buddhism took him to Scotland where three Llama monks had set up a monastery, but David balked at shaving his head and taking holy orders and returned to London after two weeks. He continued to study with a monk called Chimi Youngdong Rimpoche who lived in Hampstead, but was worried that outsiders would think that he was emulating the Beatles whose flirtation with the Maharishi Yogi had ended

Late 1960s. "Tuten-Bowie". An early publicity shot.

Opposite Page: Circa 1972/73. **Top Row:** *In dressing-room before show creating Ziggy.* **Center Panel:** *Mick Ronson doing up flies.* **Bottom Row:** *Ziggy onstage.*

Top: *Circa 1972/73. Ziggy with flower.* **Left:** *Circa 1972/73. Ziggy onstage.* **Right:** *April 1973. Ziggy hits Japan on the World Tour.*

originally written after David had spent an evening watching Stanley Kubrick's *2001 — A Space Odyssey*, and incorporated into the *Love You Till Tuesday* film since Pitt had requested some unrecorded material for the soundtrack. It was filmed with David wearing a tight fitting silver costume and sitting, like Major Tom, in a space capsule.

The lack of reportage angered David who let off steam in the direction of the blameless Ken Pitt since Calvin Mark Lee, who had been responsible for inviting the press, had bidden a hasty retreat. David had been seeing less and less of Pitt since moving in with Angela and coming under the influence of Marc Bolan and his friends. It was the Purcell Rooms show and its aftermath that heralded the beginning of the end of Pitt's relationship with David.

"He went off in a very bad temper," said Pitt.

"David and I were never really the same after that. It was a great tragedy for him because he was brilliant that night. Had the press been there, he would have had rave reviews for that performance and everything that happened to him in 1972 would have happened in 1969 instead. He went back to Bromley very disillusioned that night."

For David the sixties ended on the same note of gnawing disappointment that had haunted him since the King Bees folded. Six years hard work had resulted in five different record labels, a dozen singles, two albums, two managers, a few press cuttings and the odd film part, all of which added up to very little in terms of tangible success. Big changes were obviously needed.

"As soon as he started playing the number on the set I knew we'd got a hit going for us," said Pitt later. "The technicians stopped whatever they were doing and stood to listen. Minutes after David finished the song they were all humming it."

David, too, felt confident about *Space Oddity*, so confident, in fact, that he rushed off to play the tapes to a new friend, Marc Bolan, leader of Tyrannosaurus Rex, whom he had met through Denny Cordell's production assistant, Tony Visconti. Anxious for Bolan's approval, David was overjoyed when he, too, predicted that *Space Oddity* would be a hit.

"Bolan had tremendous influence on David at that time," said Pitt. "They played songs together and discussed music night after night. David considered Bolan an authority on pop music."

David, Bolan, Pitt and the film technicians were not wrong. On the strength of the song Ken Pitt secured yet another record deal for David — this time with Philips — and *Space Oddity*, produced by Gus Dudgeon, who was later to produce most of Elton John's best work, was released a month before David left Britain to compete in the Maltese and Italian song festivals. He won them both, but no sooner had success appeared on the horizon than tragedy struck on a personal level. In August, David's father, Hayward Jones, who had taken such a keen interest in his son's career, died of lobar pneumonia after a short illness. Mr Jones had been taken ill while David was in Italy, and David arrived home just in time to show

March 20, 1970. Bowie with mother and Angie after the wedding at Brixton Registrar Office, U.K.

1970. Contemplating the future.

Angie.

Late 1971. With Angie and son Zowie.

Changes ◄ This album is full of my changes and those of some of my friends — and I

Pretty ◄ the reaction of me to my wife being pregnant was archetypal daddy — Oh he's gonna be another Elvis

Eight ◄ This song is all that plus a dash of sci-fi — The city is a kind of high-life wart on the backside of the prairie

Life on Mars ◄ This is a sensitive young girls reaction to the Media

Kooks ◄ the baby was born and it looked like me and it looked like Angie and the song came out like - if you're gonna stay with us you're gonna grow up Bananas

Quicksand ◄ The chain reaction of moving around through the bliss and then the calamity of America produced this epic of confusion — Anyway, with my esoteric problems I could have written it in Plainview - or Dulwich.

There is a time and space level just before you go to sleep when all about you are losing theirs and a whoosh void gets you with a cacophony of thought — That's when I like to write my songs

Fill - Biff Rose song

Andy - A man of media and anti-message with a cute style.

Bob - This is how some see B.D.

Queen - A song on a Velvet Underground - Lou Reed framework about London sometimes.

Bewley - Another in the series of David Bowie confessions - Star-Trekl in a Leather Jacket

Circa 1972. Bowie's notes on the tracks from the Hunky Dory album.

his ailing father the statuette he had won. David, upset as he was, handled all the funeral arrangements himself.

On September 6, *Space Oddity* made number 48 in the charts but dropped out the following week. Continued airplay, largely due to the American moonshot, prompted Philips to relaunch the record and it re-entered the charts almost immediately. It stayed in the charts for 13 weeks, ultimately reaching number five. Six years later, re-released by RCA, *Space Oddity* reached number one, making David the only artist in the history of the charts to have a number one with the re-issue of a previous hit.

But back in 1969, with everything apparently going so well for David, the tide took a strange turn. Despite the success of *Space Oddity* and the promise it offered, David chose, for

Circa 1968/69. With perm.

reasons unknown, to shun the obvious route to stardom. Instead of capitalizing on the opportunities presented, he retreated back to Beckenham, hiding out with his new girl friend, Angela Barnett.

David had met Angie, an American design student, at a rock business party thrown by Island Records at the Speakeasy Club to launch their new signing, King Crimson. Angela's escort for the night was American record producer Lou Reisner, but she found herself sitting next to David who asked her if she could jive. They did — and within a matter of weeks the pair had set up home in Beckenham at 42, Southend Road. They were to live there together for the next four years.

The most likely reason for David's instant retreat at the turn of the decade was the reception he received on a short Scottish tour supporting Humble Pie and at a few isolated solo appearances. The reception was good, too good in fact for the inexperienced David. The screams of teenage girls and the mob scenes backstage were alien to David's fragile nature, especially as the youthful audiences seemed less interested in his music than they were in his actual physical presence.

"I would never have believed in a million years that people would scream at me," he told biographer George Tremlett at the time. "I am really incredulous. I'm receiving the most extraordinary things through the post, crucifixes, fluffy toys and weird letters from girls who promise to do strange things to me!"

If David wasn't keen to capitalize on the success of *Space Oddity*, Philips were. The record company put their ascending star back into the studio to record an album with his friend Tony Visconti producing. Titled simply *David Bowie*, the album was released in November and launched at a special concert at London's Purcell Rooms. The concert was organized by Calvin Mark Lee, an American friend of Tony Visconti's and, by all accounts, was a huge artistic success. Much to David's annoyance, no press attended to report the proceedings.

1972. Ziggy onstage.

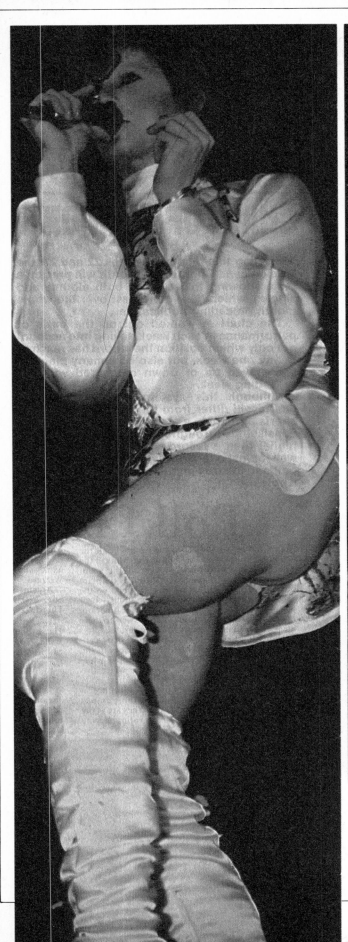

Left: *1973. Ziggy shows a leg.* **Right:** *October 17, 1973. The 1980 Floor Show at London's Marquee Club.*

TWO

1972 Tour. Ziggy.

THE ROCK WORLD had changed dramatically in the six years since David Bowie made his first hesitant steps on to record. By the beginning of the new decade the rush of excitement that followed the Beatles had been harnessed by the record companies and regulated on a more orderly — and profitable — basis. The Beatles themselves had split up in a morass of bitter legislation and their successors in the big league were determined not to make the same mistakes.

The era of the instrumental virtuoso was at hand. Eric Clapton, the blues guitarist, was hailed as 'God' by his followers; Jimmy Page stunned rock fans by inventing heavy rock and creating its ultimate vehicle in Led Zeppelin; the Who had unleashed *Tommy* on the world and dazzled audiences with the most exciting live performances ever seen on a rock stage.

Rock had grown up, matured in a way which many felt was alien to its roots. The excitement was still there and rock's audience had grown a hundredfold, but the one-shot highs had been replaced by career-orientated groups who followed a standard formula for success. Single sales were down, album sales were up; pop packages were out, groups performed for up to two hours using tons of sophisticated PA equipment. America had opened its doors to British bands and fortunes were being made by astute musicians with equally astute managers. Led Zeppelin, for one, concentrated their initial efforts on the American market. Soon rock would eclipse films and professional sport as the highest grossing branch of the entertainment industry.

If David Bowie was aware of all this in his Beckenham flat — now re-christened Haddon Hall — he didn't show it. Instead he persisted with the Arts Lab at the Three Tuns pub, hung around with Marc Bolan's set, and allowed his relationship with Ken Pitt to go from bad to worse to non-existent. Bolan's friends, Tony Visconti in particular, were distrustful of manipulative managers who collected their percentages off the backs of struggling artists. A spirit of rebellion and self-reliance was nurtured within David.

His first independent step was to record a single with Marc Bolan backed by an ad-hoc band who called themselves Hype. The line-up was Bolan on guitar, Mick 'Woody' Woodmansey on drums, Tony Visconti on bass plus a newcomer, Yorkshire born guitarist Mick Ronson who was then playing with a group called Rats. The single *The Prettiest Star*, produced by Visconti, was released on Mercury (Philips) in February and David subsequently lost the master tapes. Despite the record's star potential and Bolan's unique guitar work, it stiffed in the shops, but this embryonic band was the first grouping of David and two future Spiders.

David's second independent step was to marry Angie whose permit to stay in England was about to be revoked by the authorities. Angie's full name was Mary Angela Barnett and she was the daughter of an American mining engineer living in Cyprus. She had been educated in Switzerland and New York and had just completed a course in

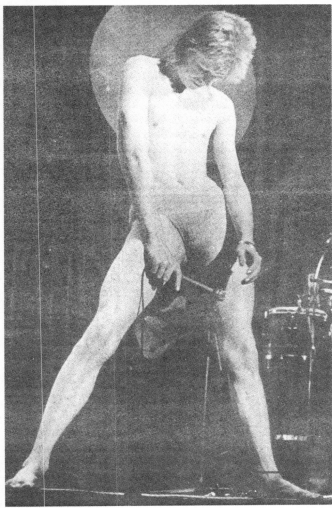
1972. On tour as Ziggy.

But first there was another album to record for Philips. *The Man Who Sold The World* was, in every respect, a massive clue to the direction that David's career would shortly take. For a start there was the cover which depicted David reclining on a bright blue chaise longue wearing a long silk dress designed by Mr Fish. It was actually a parody of a painting by pre-Raphaelite artist Dante Gabriel Rosetti but it was still strong stuff by normal standards and in the US, Mercury (Philips' American arm), balked at the controversial sleeve. They substituted a cowboy cartoon by David's old sparring partner George Underwood which displeased David so much that he made up his mind to leave the label at the earliest opportunity.

The music, too, showed signs of what was soon to come. Lyrically the songs explored pessimistic, philosophical visions of a doom-laden world edging closer to some catastrophic abyss, subject matter that would occupy more and more space on David's future records. Tony Visconti, Mick Ronson, Mick Woodmansey and Ralp Mace (synthesizer) all played on the album which was Visconti's last production collaboration with David for four years. Bolan, enjoying the first of what was to become a string of hit singles, was taking up all the American producer's time.

The Man Who Sold The World was released in November, but it made scarcely a ripple in the charts despite the public's growing fascination with this unusual artist. David himself aimed his frustration at Ken Pitt who was still attempting to mould David on traditional showbusiness lines, and this time he shared his anxiety with Olav Wyper, then heading the Philips operation in the UK. Wyper suggested that David consult a lawyer in

psychology at Kingston Polytechnic. They were married at Bromley Registry Office on March 20, 1970, with a select few of David's friends in attendance. Ken Pitt wasn't among them but David's mother, Margaret Jones, turned up uninvited after she had discovered her son's intentions by detective work. After the ceremony the small party went back to David's flat and watched television together.

David's third and ultimately most significant move was to seek out ways in which to extricate himself from his managerial contract with Ken Pitt. It was to be a slow process but in so doing David found himself a manager whose vision coincided with his own. The combination of Bowie and Tony De Fries was a devastating partnership which took David to the height of his profession in less than two years. That they would ultimately clash was inevitable.

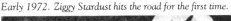
Early 1972. Ziggy Stardust hits the road for the first time.

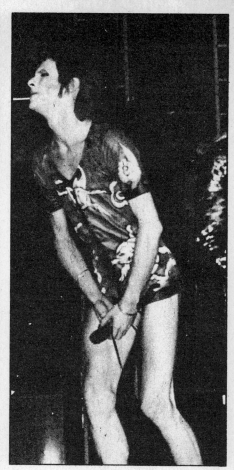

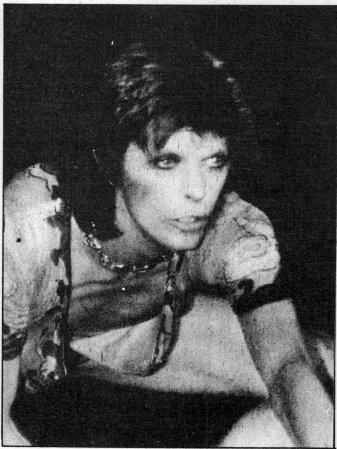

order to leave Pitt, and he recommended his own legal adviser Tony De Fries.

Born in Shepherds Bush, Tony De Fries was the son of a market trader who had gone into law with the firm of Martin Boston and Company in Wigmore Street. By 1964 he was acting as litigation clerk for record producer Mickie Most in a dispute involving the Animals, despite the fact that he wasn't registered by the Law Society as a qualified solicitor or articled clerk. For two years De Fries dispensed legal advice to Most before branching out on his own to handle the financial affairs of various London models including Vickie Hodge and Jane

Lumb. In 1969 he went into partnership with Laurence Myers at Gem, a management, production and record company, and it was at their Cavendish Square offices that David Bowie poured out his troubles.

"He came wandering in very unshaven, hollow-cheeked, bleary-eyed and nervous, chewing his fingernails and sat in my office looking like a refugee," said De Fries later. "He always looks like a refugee unless he's been properly dressed and put together for the day.

"I felt sorry for him. When David wants people to do things he usually gets people to feel sorry for him. I thought 'poor little

chap… he's got himself into a terrible mess'."

Even though there were two more years to run on his contract Pitt waived the agreement without argument after meeting with De Fries. "I had to consider the atmosphere," said Pitt. "Each of us knew we'd come to a situation. David blamed himself. He said to me 'Ken, I'm sorry, but I can't be a cause'."

All this, of course, left David without a manager, so he naturally turned to De Fries. "The next thing was he brought Angela in to see me, which is David's way of showing faith I suppose," said De Fries. "They were like a couple of children — the three year old bringing his closest

friend to see you. I've never been able to think of either of them as anything more than a couple of children."

De Fries had little knowledge of Bowie's music beyond *Space Oddity* and he spent six months listening to David's material before coming to the conclusion that he was "potentially bigger than Dylan" (as he told a dozen different record companies in the ensuing months). For his part David assembled a new band to rehearse for De Fries — Mick Ronson, Woody Woodmansey and bass player Trevor Bolder — and signed a management contract with the contractual whizz-kid. De

Late 1972. For the fashion conscious Bowie takes flared trousers to the extreme.

Fries' next move was to find a new record outlet.

RCA and CBS, both big American companies, were the two main contenders to sign the new style David Bowie on the strength of the demo tapes that would surface eventually as *Hunky Dory*. In the end CBS turned David down because company President Clive Davis had been put off by the sexually suggestive nature of the original sleeve of *The Man Who Sold The World*. "Besides," said Dan Loggins, A & R boss of CBS in London, "De Fries was asking a lot and David had just come off two loser albums on Philips."

RCA had no such scruples and they welcomed David with open arms. The deal which would give the giant American conglomerate their biggest act since Elvis Presley was signed in New York by A & R chief Dennis Katz who echoed the enthusiasm of De Fries by telling the world that Bowie is "potentially as big as Presley". De Fries glowed with pride while David prepared himself for superstardom.

With hindsight there seems to have been a massive and calculated super-sell on the part of De Fries. His persuasive talents were such that he was able to talk RCA into parting with a large sum of money for David's signature, especially since David's track record up to that point had consisted of one failed attempt after another. In fact, De Fries was only just beginning his big sell — even before David was a star in the eyes of the public (and in actual record sales) he managed to convince the record industry and the all-important but often cynical music press that his new protege was a superstar. They all believed him and, in believing, proved him to be correct.

Most of 1971 was spent in preparation for living up to De Fries' confident predictions. In February David made his first trip to the US but was unable to perform due to visa problems. Instead, he toured radio stations and talked with disc jockeys who were impressed with *The Man Who Sold The World*. While in Chicago he performed illegally at the Quiet Knight Club, appearing in his now notorious Mr Fish dress and playing acoustic guitar to a bemused, but not unsympathetic, audience. In New York David befriended Lou Reed who was embarking on a solo career after the demise of the Velvet Underground, and met artist Andy Warhol.

During the summer David (and Hype) played a few isolated shows in London and the provinces, performing songs that would soon appear on *Hunky Dory*, and in June David and Angie's son, christened Duncan Zowie Hayward, was born. The latter half of 1971 was spent at Trident Recording Studios in Soho laying down the *Hunky Dory*

Circa 1972/73.

tracks with producer Ken Scott. From the public standpoint David was in total seclusion: in reality great plans were being made for the grand re-entrance.

And grand it certainly was. To be a star, theorized De Fries, you must act like one regardless of expense. As *Hunky Dory* hit the shops in January, 1972, David invested in a wardrobe of extraordinary clothes, camp, colorful and quite unlike anything worn by pop singers before him. Bedecked in this futuristic regalia and topped by a shock of bright orange hair, David's personality changed overnight. The loser became the winner; the actual winning was just a matter of time.

What prompted his elevation of status as much as anything else was an interview with Michael Watts of the *Melody Maker* that hit the streets on January 22. Then the biggest selling and most influential music weekly in England, the *Melody Maker* was not often given to taking chances with its cover story, but Watts persuaded editor Ray Coleman to give Bowie the full treatment. Beneath the headline 'Oh You Pretty Thing' was a large photo of David in his campy culottes and an equally campy paragraph extolling his virtues and mode of operation.

Inside the magazine things went even further. "David's present image," wrote Watts, "is to come on like a swishy queen, a gorgeously effeminate boy. He's as camp as a row of tents with his limp hand and trolling vocabulary, 'I'm gay,' he says, 'and always have been, even when I was David Jones'."

And when Watts asked why David wasn't wearing his girls' dress, Bowie replied: "My dear, you must understand that it's not a woman's. It's a man's dress."

The story, which was quickly followed up by the rest of the music press, had

Circa 1972/73. Ziggy Stardust onstage.

a dynamic effect on David's career. Even before his records started selling in big numbers, every journalist in England wanted an audience with this bisexual android who was far and away the most interesting arrival on the pop scene for years.

Looking back on the episode, it is crucial to realize the important role that De Fries played in oiling the wheels of the record industry and utilizing the power of the pop press to his utmost advantage. The fact that David wasn't, isn't and never had been gay or even bisexual made not one scrap of difference to his plans and the sly, tongue-in-cheek nature of Watts' article led the reader to assume what he liked rather than simply take the admission at its word.

It was the timing of the admission, the effect it had and the manner in which De Fries orchestrated the onslaught of publicity that demonstrated the manipulative genius of his management. After all, homosexuality was fairly

common in the music industry and had been carried on behind closed doors for years; David simply used its shock value for effect. Three years later he was to deny the whole charade.

De Fries followed up the admission by witholding access to the new star, a well known managerial ploy which Colonel Tom Parker utilized with Elvis Presley and which governed Peter Grant's management of Led Zeppelin. Restriction of exposure always leaves the public wanting more — a strategy which paid off handsomely in David's case.

From that point on it was plain sailing. Like a snowball running downhill, the David Bowie phenomenon just got bigger and bigger. Driven on by De Fries' direction and RCA's cash, Bowie slaughtered the opposition by taking to the road with a revitalized stage show that utilized all the colorful and sexual gimmicks at David's command. In May a planeload of American journalists was flown over

to England at a cost of $25,000 to witness a superb concert by David and the band at Aylesbury's Friars Club where a partisan audience could be guaranteed. The touring led to the June release of *Ziggy Stardust and the Spiders From Mars*, again produced by Ken Scott at Trident, and the album became the show. With David as Ziggy and the band as The Spiders, the Royal Festival Hall was the scene for a concert which prompted the ever enthusiastic *Melody Maker* to confirm their earlier predictions. This time their cover story was headlined 'A Star Is Born' and the gushing review by editor Ray Coleman ought to have placed David in the supertax bracket for life.

By mid-1972 David was surrounded by the superstar trappings that, just over a year ago, seemed unimaginable. Chauffeur driven limousines whisked him from place to place, a personal hairdresser and make-up man were always at hand, burly bodyguards kept the press and public at bay and the swish

Dorchester Hotel was used as the setting for his increasingly infrequent interviews. What the public didn't know — and what De Fries took pains to conceal — was that David was actually still living with his wife and son in his £7 a week flat in Beckenham.

De Fries had formed a new company, Mainman, to look after David's affairs and a staff photographer was elected to point his lens exclusively at David whenever necessary. The product — and in De Fries' eyes Bowie was most definitely a product — had to be manufactured, publicized and marketed in the most productive, efficient and financially rewarding ways possible. Spontaneity was no longer appropriate; deliberately planned tactics took over. Bowie became a goldfish in a bowl while De Fries, the ringmaster, called all the shots. The only road, for all concerned, was onward.

In July and August David worked on the production

Opposite Page:
1973 U.S.A. Tour. Early Ziggy with Mick Ronson.

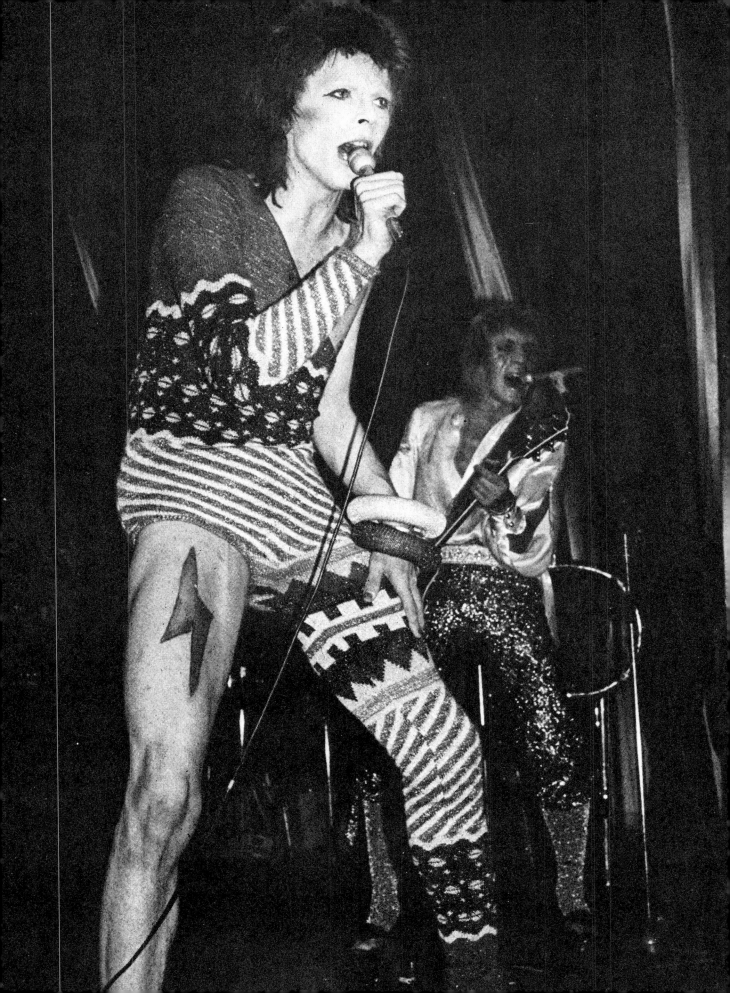

of records by Lou Reed, Iggy Pop and Mott The Hoople. In all three cases David's intervention realized hitherto unanticipated commercial rewards, the most spectacular renaissance occurring with Mott The Hoople. In their case David donated a single, *All The Young Dudes*, which rescued the struggling band from splitting up amidst a mountain of debts. The single rose to number three in the British charts and spearheaded a remarkable recovery for the band who immediately — and successfully — allied themselves with the 'glam rock' movement.

In September it was America's turn to worship at the altar. Already primed by the visiting journalists, the US fans swarmed to New York's Carnegie Hall where David made his American debut on September 28. Concerts in 13 other US cities followed before David sailed home for a Christmas concert at London's Rainbow Theatre.

It had been a busy year. The two albums had spawned three hit singles, *Starman, John I'm Only Dancing* and *The Jean Genie*, and David had performed over fifty spectacular shows with the Spiders at home and abroad. This hectic pace was to continue throughout 1973, accelerating to a frenzy of activity that culminated in the fiasco at Earls Court, the longest British tour ever undertaken by a rock star

and the much publicized 'retirement' show at Hammersmith Odeon.

The year began with another series of sessions at Trident Studios recording *Aladdin Sane*, again under the production supervision of Ken Scott. Originally titled *A Lad In Vein*, the album recruited pianist Mike Garson to the Spiders and boasted a gatefold sleeve with breathtaking portraits of David. Though it would not be released until April, *Aladdin Sane* was David's most successful album ever, advance orders in the UK reaching 150,000 and its release coinciding, once again, with an onslaught of publicity and live activity.

On January 25 David left Southampton Docks to sail for America to begin a three month world tour that put the final stamp on his international popularity. Although David had flown several times before, he became uneasy about planes in the early seventies and all his major tours were undertaken by road, rail and sea. Eventually he would fly again, but the round the world trek that occupied the first four months of 1973 was a marathon land journey that Phileas Fogg would have envied.

Amidst a great deal of pomp and ceremony David and a massive entourage crossed the USA by road and rail, sailed the Pacific for Japan and caught the Trans-Siberian Express from Vladivostok via Moscow (where they stayed to watch the May Day Parade) to Poland. The Orient Express took

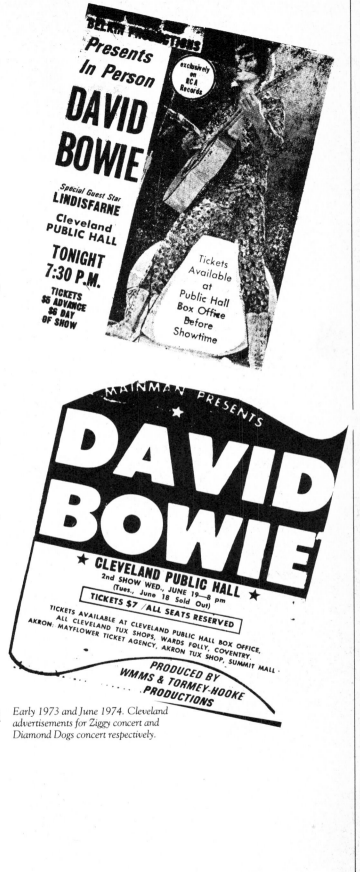

Early 1973 and June 1974. Cleveland advertisements for Ziggy concert and Diamond Dogs concert respectively.

Opposite Page:
Circa 1973. Ziggy publicity.

what remained of the party to Paris and, after a few nights at the George V hotel, David and Angie returned to England on a hovercraft. When they finally emerged at Victoria Station 300 screaming girls mobbed the couple before they could retreat to their £7 a week Beckenham outpost. "All I want to do now is go home and watch television," he told reporters waiting at the station, and who could blame him?

Along the route there had been concerts that almost brought David to his knees with exhaustion. Never the most robust specimen of manhood, David chain smokes constantly, and the endless itinerary took its toll well before he arrived back in England. David collapsed after his Valentine's Day concert at New York's Radio City Music Hall, but was on his feet again the following day to greet a tribe of Japanese journalists. To avoid unnecessary press harassment a press liaisonette had been appointed by De Fries in the form of underground actress Cherry Vanilla whose job it was to talk to journalists about David, his likes and dislikes, his views and opinions. Later she was to admit: "We peddled David's ass like there was no tomorrow," but for the time being she was yet another colorful character to add to David's retinue.

The American and Japanese shows were beefed up musically with the

1973, U.S.A. "Ziggy played guitar".

addition of horns, guitar and percussion and the material performed consisted primarily of tracks from *Ziggy Stardust* and the soon-to-be released *Aladdin Sane*. When the tour stopped off at Tokyo on April 15, the audience were astonished at the theatrical nature of the shows, barely comprehending what was occurring before their eyes. By the time David reached London again he had been

Early 1973. On tour as Aladdin Sane.

away for exactly one hundred days, twenty more than Mr Fogg, but the concerts had proved even more gruelling than rescuing an Indian Princess.

"I've gone through a lot of changes on my way back from Japan," he told rock writer Roy Hollingworth who accompanied the Bowies on the last leg of their journey from Paris to London and who reported that David was as sick as a dog. "After what I've seen of the state of the world I've never been so damned scared in my life. If I wrote about it, it would be my last album ever because I don't think I'd be around very long after finishing it."

Bowie admitted to Hollingworth that the tour had been a great strain on his health and that he was aware that he had been the victim of a massive sales campaign which had paid off on a scale he found quite unbelievable. "I have become disillusioned with

certain things," he said. "I never believed a hype could be made of an artist before he got anywhere. That's what happened and I don't like it. But when I saw that our albums were really selling... that's when I knew the hype was over. Well... it wasn't over but at least we'd done something to be hyped about.

"The whole hype thing at the start was a monster to endure. It hurt me quite a lot. I had to go through a lot of crap. I never thought Ziggy would become the most talked about man in the world."

And David dropped a hint that Ziggy's days would soon be numbered. "I became Ziggy on stage. That was my ego, but I don't think Ziggy is my ego anymore. It's a more mature David Bowie now," he said.

But fortune smiles on the brave, and David's return to London coincided with *Aladdin Sane* reaching number one in the album charts. Eight days later David and the Spiders performed their first British concert of the year before 18,000 fans at the Earls Court exhibition hall, an event which went down in history as the worst example of a bad deal in the history of British rock. It was a complete fiasco, ruined by poor acoustics, non-existent sight lines and a drunken audience who danced naked and urinated in the aisles. David stopped the show at

Opposite Page:
March 1973. Ziggy onstage, transforming into Aladdin Sane.

Early 1973. Publicity for Aladdin Sane.

one point to plead with the audience to remain calm, but violence broke out again and again as the mob surged towards the stage. A second Earls Court concert, scheduled for June 30, was canceled for fear of a repetition and David, De Fries and the promoters drew a veil over the entire affair.

A week later David began the biggest concert tour Britain had ever seen with over 150,000 eager fans packing into 40 odd venues from Aberdeen to Torquay. Every seat had been sold out weeks in advance and *Life On Mars*, a single taken from *Aladdin Sane* reached number three in the charts in mid tour.

The runaway juggernaut had to stop somewhere and David chose to bury Ziggy

Stardust on stage at the Hammersmith Odeon on July 4 — the last stop of the tour. The announcement came immediately after crack guitarist Jeff Beck had joined Bowie on stage for a steamy jam at the end of *Jean Genie*. Bowie took the microphone and stated: "Of all the shows on the tour this one will remain with us the longest because not only is it the last show of the tour but it's the last show we'll ever do."

The audience reacted by screaming "No" at the top of their voices and some even broke into tears, but David was adamant. What he actually meant, of course, was that the Ziggy Stardust show was not to be repeated, that it was the last show he would perform with the Spiders as his

backing unit. Since this wasn't made clear, the spectacle of Bowie abandoning his career made headlines in the press and it took weeks before the situation was clarified.

After the Hammersmith show a massive party was thrown at the Café Royal in Regent Street with a guest list that read like a who's who of showbusiness: Mick and Bianca Jagger, Paul and Linda McCartney, Ringo and Maureen Starr, Keith Moon, Barbra Streisand, Sonny Bono, Tony Curtis, Elliott Gould, Ryan O'Neil, Peter Cook, Dudley Moore, Jeff Beck, the Spiders and a host of lesser known brethren. Film director Richard Pennebaker, who had flown to London to film the final show, was also present but his work that evening never saw the light of day. Neither did the live recording made by RCA.

Word of the party leaked and crowds gathered in Regent Street that night to gasp at the celebrities alighting from their limousines to sip champagne with David. In slightly less than two years he had joined the elite ranks of bona fide superstars, but disenchantment with stardom was creeping up on Bowie fast.

With or without De Fries' agreement, David canceled a proposed American tour and subsequently announced that he had more important things to do with his life than continue the never-ending series of tours to promote albums. The day after "retiring" David and Angie caught the boat train to Paris for a short rest before beginning work on his next album, *Pin Ups*. It was the end of Ziggy, and David undoubtedly gave a massive sigh of relief.

Early 1973. Aladdin Sane onstage.

Circa 1973. Offstage.

THREE

February/March 1973. Aladdin Sane Tour, U.S.A.

BY THE END of 1973 David Bowie was the most interesting British rock star to have emerged in the seventies. On an international level the only other contenders were Elton John and Rod Stewart, both equally flamboyant in appearance but lacking the aura of mystique that David — thanks mainly to De Fries — had managed to cultivate. Also John and Stewart were rock stars pure and simple: Bowie had other cards up his satin sleeve.

Thus 'glam-rock' (aka 'glitter-rock') was credited as Bowie's invention. It is a spurious term that loosely incorporated any artist whose stage apparel went beyond the standard uniform of faded blue jeans and tee-shirts. Marc Bolan, Slade, Gary Glitter, Mott The Hoople and even The Sweet were all considered part of the movement but, Mott aside, Bowie actually had little influence on these performers. His influence extended more to the art rock school that was growing up in New York as a simplistic antithesis of another breed, the pomp rockers, on whom Bowie had no influence whatsoever. The gaudy, overdressed New York Dolls, with their camp appearance and crude music, felt Bowie's influence strongly, and their brand of idealism was to make itself felt more and more as the decade progressed.

On the other side of the Atlantic David was about to record a stop-gap album of songs by artists whose music had played a formative role in his musical education. As David's albums go, *Pin Ups* ranks poorly in artistic achievement, but it is a sincere tribute to many of the groups who appeared at the Marquee Club at around the same period as David. Included on *Pin Ups* are songs by the Who, the Pretty Things, Pink Floyd, Them, the Kinks, the Yardbirds, the Mojos, the Easy Beats and the Merseybeats. The last named wrote *Sorrow*, which RCA released as a single to coincide with the album's release in October. It made number three in the British charts.

Pin-Ups was recorded at the Chateau d'Herouville outside Paris, and drummer Aynsley Dunbar, a noted session player, was brought in to replace Woody Woodmansey from the Spiders. The two other original Spiders, Mick Ronson and Trevor Bolder, recorded with David for the

Opposite Page:
1973. On tour as Ziggy.

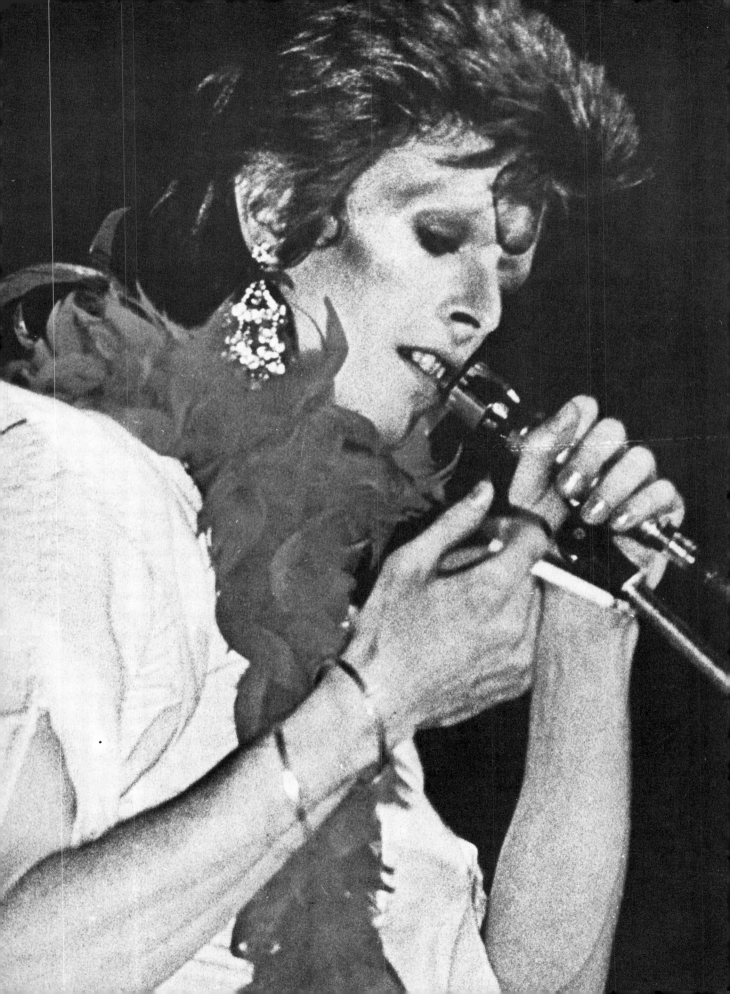

February 1973. U.S.A. Tour. With Lou Reed and Iggy Pop in New York (Tony De Fries in background).

last time on these sessions, though Mike Garson would remain with David for another two years. The sleeve of *Pin-Ups* featured David alongside Twiggy, the fashion model.

Returning to London, David made his last appearance as Ziggy Stardust with the Spiders at the Marquee Club on October 17 and 18 in a show that was recorded for NBC, the American TV channel, and broadcast on their Midnight Special TV show a month later. It was never shown in England, but isolated clips were used to promote singles. Titled *The 1980 Floor Show*, the extravaganza featured

David with the musicians who had worked on *Pin-Ups* plus Marianne Faithfull (with whom David duetted on *I Got You Babe*) and the Troggs whose recording of *Wild Thing* remains a classic to this day. The audience was democratically selected by ballot amongst members of the newly formed International David Bowie Fan Club — another Mainman venture with an eye to increased profits.

For the remainder of the year David took a well earned rest from public activities. The pressure of stardom forced him to move from Haddon Hall in Beckenham to Kensington

where he and Angie rented the home of actress Diana Rigg before selecting a home of their own in the same locality. It was a period in which Angie came increasingly out of her shell, modeling for British tabloids in clothes of her own design and emphasizing the unisex looks that she and David epitomized. They posed together in shots where only David's stature identified him from his wife; they were the Space Age couple, light years ahead of their growing legion of followers.

The first two months of 1974 were taken up with the recording of *Diamond*

Dogs in London and Hilversum, in Holland. This album saw the return of Tony Visconti as David's producer, a partnership that has remained intact to the present day. Herbie Flowers, the most accomplished session bassist in England, was drafted in to replace Trevor Bolder, and another session stalwart, Tony Newman, shared the percussion duties with Aynsley Dunbar. Mike Garson was retained on keyboards and David himself played guitar as well as saxophone and synthesizer. Mick Ronson, hard at work in his unsuccessful attempt to become a star in his own right, was barely missed.

David had originally intended to write a musical based on George Orwell's book *1984*, but was refused permission by the author's widow. Nevertheless the album steers the same course as Orwell's epic: the breakdown of civilization, empty cities patrolled by oversized rats and an all pessimistic view of the future of mankind. But the songs were pure rock and roll. *Rebel Rebel* was a match for the Rolling Stones anyday and the sleeve, designed by Rock Dreams artist Guy Peellaert, was a knockout. *Diamond Dogs* became another huge seller for David.

March and April were spent in New York, roaming the clubs and rehearsing the band who would soon take to the road

his retirement from the rock stage at the Hammersmith Odeon last year. For the act that David puts over on this tour has as much to do with rock 'n' roll as Bob Dylan has with Las Vegas.

"The one-and-a-half-hour long, 20-song show is a completely rehearsed and choreographed routine where every step and nuance has been perfected down to the last detail. There isn't one iota of spontaneity about the whole show.

"It is straight off a musical stage — a piece of theater complete with extravagant mechanical sets, dancers and a band

that stands reservedly to stage right and never even receives a cursory acknowledgement, like an orchestra in a theatre pit.

"The show belongs on Broadway or Shaftesbury Avenue rather than on the road. The whole concept takes a complete turn around from what a rock audience anticipates, but at Toronto on Sunday it left them stunned. Perhaps the crowd at the O'Keefe Theater literally couldn't believe their eyes.

"Fittingly there was no encore and the applauding audience was greeted with the announcement ten minutes after the show stopped that Bowie

had already left the theater. The Colonel Parker touch in manager Tony De Fries is always there.

"The music actually appears secondary to the various effects and dance routines and while it could be argued that Alice Cooper has taken rock theater to its extreme level, Bowie has moved on to a totally different level with this show.

"It was more in the vein of a Liza Minelli performance, or even a Vegas night club cabaret. A Christmas pantomime would be an unfair parallel, but the ideas behind it were exactly the same.

"Bowie comes out of this show as some kind

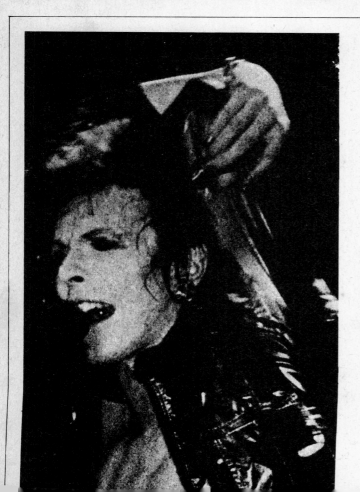

of magical being. A star above stars, as untouchable as the sky. Not once does he address the audience, or even allude to their presence other than an odd grin. Each song is linked together so that no delays occur during the show, and he doesn't even take a bow at the end.

"The material is a sensible mixture of songs from the *Diamond Dogs* album and assorted old favourites. The backing band — Earl Slick, an American guitarist, Herbie Flowers on bass, Mike Garson from the old Spiders, on keyboards, and Tony Newman on drums — are first class, note perfect to an almost mechanical degree. Their presence

which rises and falls at Bowie's command. Three equally high lighting towers, cunningly disguised as skyscrapers, beam down on the star of the show. Illustrated at the left of the stage is a kind of phallic symbol spurting blood towards the sky. The band are off to the right.

"Throughout the entire show Bowie goes through a series of well rehearsed dance steps and mimes to act out each song in the persona of the character involved. The expanse of unoccupied stage in the centre is ample for all manner of complex choreography involving chairs, ropes and sundry other props.

"The opening song was *1984*. Bowie was

Top Right: *Summer 1974, U.S.A. On the Diamond Dogs Review.* **Bottom Left:** *Summer 1974, U.S.A. On the Diamond Dogs Review.* **Top Left:** *Autumn 1973. Photo session to promote "Pin-Ups".* **Bottom Right:** *1974. Onstage in America on the Soul Tour.*

May 1, 1973. In Red Square, Moscow, before returning to England by land via Japan.

catwalk for the first time, dressed in a long trench coat and gazing down on the dancers below while singing and pouting. Yellow lamp standards up on the wall gave the song an eerie but sad atmosphere.

"Eventually the huge bridge machinery swung into motion rather like Tower Bridge opening to allow a steamer to pass through. Bowie was lowered between the two pillars to land safely back in the centre of the stage.

"Next song was *Changes*, with more dance routines, then *Suffragette City, All The Young Dudes* and *Will You Rock And Roll With Me*, which appeared to close the first sequence of the performance. Houselights went up and for the first time Bowie bent to receive his applause.

"*Watch That Man* began phase two, followed by *Drive In Saturday* on which David played guitar for the first and only time during the show. As the opening chords of *Space Oddity* thundered from Earl Slick's guitar, Bowie appeared to have left the arena, but then a door atop one of the skyscrapers swung open to reveal him on a seat on a pole — actually a hydraulic boom expanding from the base of the phallic symbol.

"David began the song perched up there, singing into what appeared to be a hand-held telephone, but as the verses progressed and David took on the identity of Major Tom, the boom moved forward and extended diagonally outwards so that he was projected somewhat precariously out above the front rows of the audience. Complete with flashing lights everywhere the effect was nothing short

July 4, 1973. The Cafe Royal party on Regent Street, London, following Bowie's "retirement".

of sensational.

"From then on the various effects were difficult to comprehend in one short viewing. To grasp every detail one would have to watch at least three shows.

"At one stage (during *Diamond Dogs*) David was tied up in ropes by the dancers, and at another point he was in the centre of a boxing ring, wearing boxing gloves, to sing *Panic In Detroit*. He even had a big black dude walk on in a track suit to act as his second, toweling him down and fitting a fresh gum shield between verses.

"But even these effects paled in comparison to the Houdini-like routine during the last half hour. For this David appeared perched above a platform of mirrors wheeled on from the rear. The platform turned out to be a gigantic square box rather like some conjuror's lavish prop, into which Bowie descended and disappeared from view. The front doors of the box were opened by his dancers but... no David. Just a gigantic sparkling black hand against ultra-violet strip lights. Eventually the hand lowered to reveal a glittering staircase for Bowie to take the stage once more.

"For the final medley of *Jean Genie* and *Rock And Roll*

Suicide, a tiny but powerful spot at the base of the stage was switched on to create giant shadows of David and the dancers which loomed eerily over the painted metropolis on the backdop.

"The show was over before you knew it. Suddenly the audience were yelling for more at a stage which had emptied in seconds. It was the most original spectacle in 'rock' I've ever seen, a complete

step forward for Bowie and pop in general.

"Quite how much the settings, machinery, rehearsals and transportation must have cost in man-hours and money is anybody's guess, but it seems doubtful whether David will be singing a bill for less than six figures, and this may go some way towards explaining the unusually high ticket price for a rock concert.

August 1973. In France, during the recording of "Pin-Ups".

"But David Bowie circa 1974 is not rock any more. He can only be described as an entertainer who looks further ahead than any other in rock, and whose far-reaching imagination has created a combination of contemporary music and theatre that is several years ahead of its time."

The *Diamond Dogs Revue* visited 28 more venues before winding up at New York's Madison Square Garden on July 19. In larger venues — the Garden holds 20,000 people — many of the nuances contained in the presentation were lost in the vastness of the auditoria, but this was far from the only problem encountered by David. The practical difficulty in moving the enormous set from place to place was proving to be too much for the crew to handle, and in Tampa the show was performed without the effects because a truck driver failed to arrive on time. Overworked roadies — there were 15 of them — and malfunctioning equipment contributed to the headaches, and a threatened strike by the backing band almost sank the two Philadelphia shows which were recorded for the *David Live* album.

The labor dispute was an omen for David's future disenchantment with Mainman, for Tony De Fries had refused to increase the salaries of the musicians beyond the basic minimum set down by the Musicians Union. In the

The "retirement" party.

end David coughed up the difference from his own pocket — but the seeds of financial discontent were obviously being sown. Either way the *Diamond Dogs Revue* was grinding to a halt under its own weight.

In August, during a break in the touring schedule, David checked into the Sigma Sound Studios in Phildelphia to begin work on what would become *Young Americans*, his 'blue-eyed soul' album, and at the beginning of September the Revue was staged for a week at the Los Angeles Universal Amphitheater before the props were packed away for good. England — or anywhere else outside the US and Canada — would never see Bowie's most lavish stage production.

"I think I always know when to stop doing something," David told Robert Hilburn of the *Los Angeles Times* during his stint in LA. "It's when the enjoyment is gone. That's why I've changed so much. I've never been of the opinion that it's necessarily a wise thing to keep on a successful streak if you're just duplicating all the time.

1973. With Angie.

*Oh You Pretty Things
Don't you know
you're driving your
Mamas and Papas insane*

"That's why I tend to be erratic. It's not a matter of being indulgent. Everything I do I get bored with eventually. It's knowing where to stop. I have now done what I wanted to do three or four years ago.

Stage an elaborate colorful show… a fantasy… and I don't think I want to go any further with it because I know it can be done.

"I know I could do a bigger, even grander production, but when I know it can be done I don't have to do it any more. Doing a straight show is very exciting to me now: suddenly jumping into a new kind of tour after this one. I couldn't imagine just doing the same show over and over again. It would be terribly boring. That's why I 'retired' the last time."

So the touring continued without the props, taking in a further 21 cities across the US and revisiting others with a pared-down version of the *Diamond Dogs* format that subsequently became known as the Soul Tour. The shift in musical direction reflected David's recurring interest in soul and disco rhythms: on these shows the Mike

om Right: *1975. Relaxing in Los Angeles.* **Top Right:** *1976. On the first
Light Tour, U.S.A.* **Top Left:** *1976. On the first White Light Tour,
A.* **Bottom Left:** *1978. Bowie starts to perform 'German' work, ''Low''
Heroes'', which he produces with Eno.*

Garson Band warmed up the audience with a selection of soul numbers and David utilized a six-member back-up chorus. Midway through the tour the *David Live* album was released which included the soul classic *Knock On Wood*, and David previewed a few songs from *Young Americans* as the cities flashed by. The tour, which had opened on June 14, ended on December 2 in Tuscaloosa, Alabama — a mammoth itinerary by any standards. David would not tour again until 1976.

That these 'soul' shows were performed and received with equal enthusiasm was a testimony to Bowie's increasing artistic confidence and the reality of his talent. The ballyhoo that followed his Ziggy Stardust era had well and truly died down by this time and any element of hype had completely disappeared. Bowie had apparently decided that where there is truth there is no need for exaggeration, and that his talents alone would carry the show from now on. He was, as he has been ever since, quite correct.

At the end of 1974 David settled in Los Angeles, appeared on the Dick Cavett TV show and immersed himself in his latest hobby, video recording, while Angie took to the road with a lecture-entertainment show for colleges. Further sessions for *Young Americans* took place at the Electric Ladyland Studios in New York during January and it was

1973. Meditating on the price of fame?

here in Greenwich Village that John Lennon stopped by to lend his substantial talents to his own *Across the Universe* as well as the disco-styled *Fame* which was to give David his first number one in the US singles charts later in the year.

David's relationship with Lennon was fruitful in other areas too. A veteran of contractual litigation, the former Beatle was immersed in managerial law-suits with Allan Klein at the time, and had come to the conclusion that his affairs would be in better order if he managed himself. David, who by this time was at loggerheads with De Fries, took Lennon's advice and commenced legal proceedings against his manager.

Though the details of the legal dispute between

David and Tony De Fries were never made public, observers later reported that Bowie's grievances were concerned solely with the financial aspect of their relationship. After De Fries had taken a percentage of Bowie's gross earnings, the costs of the operation — touring, recording, Mainman, wages and office accommodation rents — were paid for out of the remainder. With such an extravagant budget, the net proceeds that David ultimately received were, by all accounts, paltry. David reckoned he deserved more, and appointed a Los Angeles attorney, Michael Lippman, to act on his behalf. The relationship was duly severed — but De Fries, in the opinion of various people connected with Mainman, disappeared from the scene a richer man than David.

David was certainly concerned about his financial situation at this

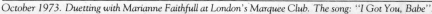

October 1973. Duetting with Marianne Faithfull at London's Marquee Club. The song: "I Got You, Babe".

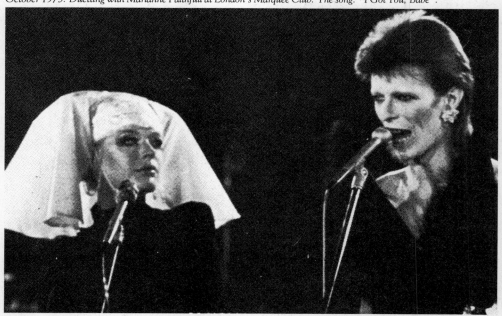

Summer 1974, U.S.A. On the road with the Diamond Dogs Review.

1974. With Stevie Wonder in New York.

time, and on his next tour he was to admit that financial considerations were his biggest motive for touring again. The Mainman offices in New York and London, once havens of extravagant activity, soon closed their doors, and *Young Americans*, released in March 1975, was the last Bowie album to carry the Mainman logo.

With Michael Lippman acting as his temporary manager, David took off for New Mexico in the summer to star in his first major film. There had been some confusion over Bowie's intentions as far as a film role was concerned: at first it was announced he would star in a film of Robert Heinlein's book *Stranger In A Strange Land*, and then in the film of Jack Higgins' best selling war novel *The Eagle Has Landed*. In the end it turned out to be *The Man Who Fell To Earth*, based on a sci-fi book by Walter Trevis, and directed by Nicolas Roeg.

The story is similar to Heinlein's book. It involves an alien, played by Bowie, who lands in America seeking aid for his family on their barren planet. With a scientific knowledge far advanced of the earthly scientists, the alien amasses great wealth through patenting his inventions and eventually finances his own personal space mission which is abandoned at the last minute due to government intervention.

Bowie's performance in the film assured its box office success, but his acting was wooden and the script's lack of continuity left movie audiences with too many unanswered questions. June, July and August were spent making the film, and the hot New Mexico sun tanned David's skin to a deep brown that showed up well on a spot on the Cher TV show in September, and on the British Russell Harty show, via satellite, in November.

Still ensconced in Los Angeles, David recorded his next album, *Station To Station*, at Cherokee Studios, with the band that accompanied him on the *Diamond Dogs Revue*: Mike Garson, Herbie Flowers and either Tony Newman or Aynsley Dunbar on the drum rostrum. Originally titled *The Return Of The Thin White Duke*, it's release came at a time when Bowie's personal life was in a turmoil. His relationship with Angie was on the rocks, and life in Los Angeles, surrounded by the rock jet-set, was having a bad effect. Too much cocaine was turning David into a vegetable, and an interview with *Rolling Stone* magazine, in which he expressed sympathy with fascist politics, had a disturbing effect on fans. Around Christmas, 1975, he realized a change of environment was essential.

"I surrounded myself with people who indulged my ego," he said later. "They treated me as though I was Ziggy Stardust or one of my characters, never realizing that David Jones might be behind it. I had a more than passing relationship with drugs… actually I was zonked out of

David Bowie: A Profile 47

1974. Publicity of Bowie with Lulu during the recording of Lulu's version of "The Man Who Sold the World".

my mind. You can do good things with drugs, but then comes a long decline.

"One winter's day, three days before Christmas, a friend pulled me over to the mirror and said 'Look at us both. If you continue to be the way you are at the moment, you'll never see me again. You're not worth the effort.' After that I locked all my characters away forever."

January, 1976, was spent in Jamaica rehearsing for a new tour with a new band: Stacey Haydon and Carlos Alomar on guitars, Tony Kaye (an original member of Yes) on keyboards, George Murray on bass and Dennis Davis on drums. Earl Slick would have joined the band but he was now managed by Michael Lippman with whom David was no longer on friendly terms. At this stage in his career David had decided to dispense with the services of a manager altogether, and handle all the aspects of his career himself with the aid of a small team of professionals who would follow his directions. Chief among these was — and still is — Pat Gibbons, an American who had the onerous task of tour managing the

Diamond Dogs Revue. Multilingual Corinne Schwab — known to all as Co-Co — was retained from Mainman as David's personal assistant, a position she still holds.

The new tour opened on February 2, 1976, in Vancouver and visited 33 North American cities before moving to Europe and eventually London for four concerts at the Wembley Empire Pool in May. It was Bowie at his most professional, with a slick band, a slick all-white light show and an even slicker program which reached back into his past for material as well as including new songs from *Young Americans* and *Station To Station*. David appeared on stage dressed in a stylish white dress shirt, a black waistcoat (with a box of Gitane cigarettes visible in one pocket) and black slacks. No longer isolated from the audience as he was in his Ziggy and Diamond

Dog days, David's manner was as warm and inviting as a cabaret performer.

When the tour reached Detroit, on March 1, I interviewed David at length in his room at the Ponchartrain Hotel. It was a wide-ranging conversation covering subjects as diverse as his bisexuality, money, right-wing politics, Lou Reed, soul music, acting and his loathing of Los Angeles. Here are some of the things he said:

"I'm just doing this tour for the money. I never earned any money before, but this time I'm going to make some. I think I deserve it, don't you?"

"The other tours were misery, so painful. I had amazing amounts of people on the road with me. I had a management system that had no idea what it was doing and which

In the recording studio with Lulu.

December 1978. Far Eastern Tour, performing his 'German' work.
Bottom Center: *1979. Bowie in drag times three for the video of "Boys Keep Swinging", a track from the "Lodger" album which is released in August.*

was totally self-interested and pompous. I was getting all the problems every night. Ten or 15 people would be coming to see me and laying their problems on me because the management couldn't or wouldn't deal with it. For me, touring was no fun at all, so the two major tours I did were horrendous experiences. I hated every minute of them, so I used to say I'd never tour again. Then I would be talked into doing it again to make somebody else some money."

"This is the most efficient tour I've ever seen. If I'm in charge I'll tour again, whereas before I always thought there was somebody better at doing this kind of thing. It wasn't until John Lennon pointed it out to me that I realized maybe the artist is as good at managing as anybody else. It was John who sorted me out all down the line. He took me on one side, sat me down and told me what it was all about, and I realized I was very naive. I still thought you had to have somebody else who dealt with

these things called contracts, but now I have a better understanding of showbusiness business."

"The right wing politics thing was just bullshit, something I said off the cuff. Some paper wanted me to say something and I didn't have much to say so I made things up. They took it all in."

"I haven't lived properly in America. I've been here but I haven't lived. I've been in Los Angeles coping with a town that I consider to be the most repulsive wart on the backside of humanity. I'd rather live here in Detroit than in Los Angeles."

"I'm enjoying this tour so I'll do some more tours. Albums? I'll make some commercial albums and I'll make some that possibly aren't as commercial. I'll probably keep alternating, providing myself with a hit album to make the money to do the next album which probably won't sell as well."

"My affairs have been so badly messed up that I haven't had time to go back to England recently. I was told I couldn't go back to England because I had tax problems there and didn't have the money to pay them, but now I do so I'm going

March 1974. The Grammy Awards, New York. After making a presentation to Aretha Franklyn for Best R&B Singer.

March 1974. Left to right: David Bowie, Art Garfunkel, Paul Simon, Yoko Ono, John Lennon and Roberta Flack, at the Grammy Awards Ceremony.

Opposite Page:
William Burroughs, the Beat Godfather and author of novels like "Nova Express", "The Wild Boys" and "Cities of the Red Night", interviews David Bowie in Rolling Stone, February 28, 1974. William Burroughs developed the Cut-Up technique of writing (first used by friend Brion Gysin) which Bowie adopts to write the lyrics for "Diamond Dogs".

June 1974. On tour with the Diamond Dogs.

know. Whether they expect theater from me or not I don't know or even care. The audiences are always about one tour behind me, but then they always were. I'd get worried if they turned up in outfits that I'd never seen before. I'd think I was a tour behind.''

''I haven't kept a band together since the Spiders and I don't want the responsibility of keeping one. It's too much money, anyway, to keep a band together... a lot of problems that I don't need.''

''My own recent music has been good, plastic soul. It's not very complex but it's enjoyable to write. I did most of it in the studio. With *Young Americans* I thought I'd better make a hit album to cement myself over here so I went in and did it. It wasn't too hard really.''

''It was John Lennon's influence that made *Fame* really, rather than his writing. There's always a lot of adrenalin flowing when John is around, but his chief addition to the song was his high pitched singing. The riff came from Carlos Alomar and the melody and most of the lyrics came from me, but it wouldn't have happened if John hadn't been there. He was the

energy and that's why he got a credit for writing it. He was the inspiration.''

''I think I've done things that I needed to do in rock 'n' roll, and I've decided that a purely rock 'n' roll career doesn't interest me. Once you've made the initial impact, what else do you do... survive? I'm just picking up on other things that have fascinated me. Over the past year I've done several silk screens and lithographs. As soon as a rock 'n' roller becomes an archetype, he has served his purpose.''

''I'm not dis-enchanted because I always believed when I started with Ziggy, for me, that was what it was all about. I said it with Ziggy five years ago and I believe that you can go up or down or be carried along by the tide for a few years. The only thing to do if you want to contribute to culture, or politics, or music, or whatever, is to utilize your own persona rather than just one medium which, in my case, has been music. The best way to do this is to diversify and become a nuisance everywhere.''

''The success of *Fame* put the cap on things. It told me I could finish now, pack it all in if I wanted. That meant I had done the

back. Unfortunately I'm going to have to live in Switzerland because I want to keep my money.''

''I never saw any money from the Diamond Dogs tour. I'm only making money now. That's why I wanted to simplify things this time around, to make money. I'm managing myself now simply because I've got fed up with the managers I've known.''

''This tour is more theatrical than Diamond Dogs ever was. It's by suggestion rather than by over-propping. Whether the audiences are aware of it, I don't

Top Right: *Early 1980. Photo which appears on the single's bag of "Crystal Japan", released in Japan as an A-side and as a B-side on the UK single "Up the Hill Backwards" (released early 1981).* **Top Left:** *1981. Promotional portrait for "Scary Monsters" album.* **Bottom:** *October 1980. Bowie as the Elephant Man onstage at New York's Booth Theater.*

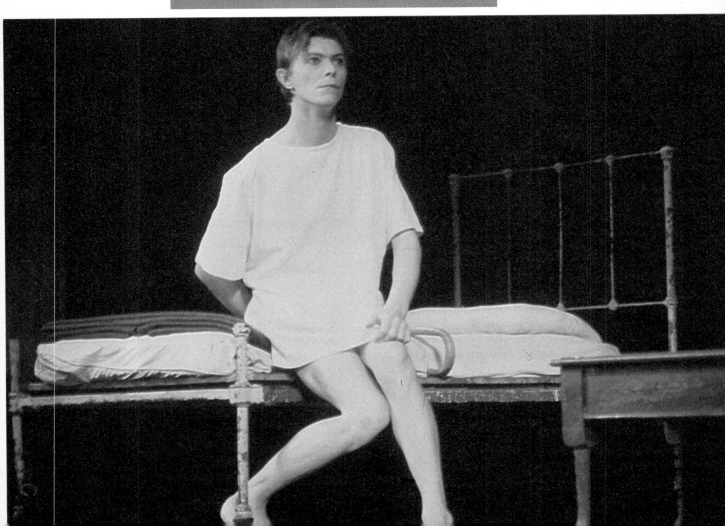

1974. *Performing on the Diamond Dogs Tour.*

two things I was supposed to do which is to conquer this (the US) market and to conquer the British market. Once you've done that you can pretend to rest on your laurels and all the other cliches you can do when you reach the top. But you can forget longevity and all the other things that make you stay there as far as I'm concerned. All that staying at the top is just a heartache for me. I just want to do what *I* want to do and, first, that's make some money with this tour and enjoy making it at the same time.''

''Bisexual? Oh Lord no. Positively not. That was just a lie. They gave me that image so I stuck to it pretty well for a few years. I never adopted that stance. It was given to me. I've never done a bisexual action in my life, on stage, on record or anywhere else. I don't think I even had much of a gay following. A few glitter queens maybe, but nothing much really. A lot of people provide me with quotes. They suggest all kinds of things to say and I do, really, because I'm not very hip at all. Then I go away and spout it all out and that makes it easier for people to classify me. People dissect the songs and say that's influenced by someone or other, but I don't know whether I've been influenced. All I know is I'm drinking a beer and enjoying myself."

When David arrived in London for the Wembley shows, his flirtation with fascism backfired. Dressed in a brown shirt with blonde hair swept completely back, he certainly resembled an Aryan superman as he stepped from a train at Victoria Station. With the National Front making an odious name for itself in British politics, it was all very unfortunate when the national press cameraman snapped David giving what appeared to be a fascist salute from his open car. "He caught me in mid wave," David said later, but the inappropriate press that greeted his homecoming undeniably soured the visit.

The concerts, though, were superb. *Melody Maker* hailed Bowie with the headline "David The Goliath/The Messiah Returns" and the critics were full of praise for his stunning stage show. Backstage at Wembley, David encountered Brian Eno, one time keyboard player with Roxy Music and latterly an avant-garde minimalist composer much liked by serious critics. The pair hit it off immediately, and David persuaded Eno to go to Berlin with him where they could make music which was in line with David's experimental visions. Utilizing Eno's ideas and techniques, David embarked on a cycle of albums totally different from anything he had recorded before.

September 1974. Onstage on the Soul Tour.

FOUR

September/October 1974. The Soul Tour, introducing the "Young American".

A WIND OF CHANGE blew through British rock in 1976, bringing with it a host of new bands trading under the punk-rock banner, and a shift in attitudes towards established rock heroes. It was inevitable that a new generation of teenagers would seek out new bands to idolize, and their quest was answered with the arrival of the short-lived but hugely influential Sex Pistols.

The Sex Pistols and their ilk were discovered first by the fans, then by the music press and finally by a reluctant record industry with independent labels leading the way, and the punk movement shattered the myth that musicians had to be virtuoso instrumentalists to make headway in rock. Characterized by off-key singing, rudimentary guitar work, basic drumming and a thoroughly anti-social political stance verging on anarchy, the Sex Pistols, aided and abetted by their manipulative manager Malcolm McLaren, barnstormed their way into the public gaze and opened the doors for dozens of imitators.

Concurrent with the rise of the punk movement was a surge of resentment towards successful career orientated groups and artists who flaunted their wealth, overindulged in drugs and enjoyed lifestyles far removed from what remained of their street following. This resentment found its voice in the British music press, notably the fast rising *New Musical Express* where a proliferation of young writers with leftish leanings leaped on the political bandwagon to score points at the expense of Rod Stewart, Led Zeppelin, Yes, Jethro Tull, Emerson Lake and Palmer and other well entrenched artists whose current output relied heavily on yesterday's glories. By and large, the fans of these groups stayed loyal, but the verbal swords were drawn; after all, no-one likes to be called a boring old fart.

Few established bands escaped the wrath of the music press. Pete Townshend, forever a seeker of truth, managed it, as did Keith Richard of the Rolling Stones, a model for punks everywhere. But no-one amongst his contemporaries managaed to retain his artistic respect as much as David Bowie. The new generation of fans — and writers — looked up to Bowie as a guiding light which, indeed, he was. As always Bowie relished in the opportunity for change and the musical climate of 1977 was ideal for his Berlin musings that appeared on *Low*, the first of his trilogy of albums with Brian Eno.

David moved to Berlin in the summer of 1976, shortly after the end of his tour. RCA, correctly sensing a lull in Bowie product, compiled *Changesonebowie* which was released in May, the first 'greatest hits' package from their star artist. Bowie's relationship with RCA, especially in America, has never been good and it seems unlikely that he was consulted regarding this release. It was aimed directly at the new fans picked up on the recent tour and through

Harlan Ellison, who has received more science fiction, screen and literature awards than any other living writer, has influenced many contemporary rock performers including Frank Zappa, Talking Heads, Gary Numan and Devo. "Diamond Dogs" borrows in part from the post-apocalyptic scenario of Ellison's story "A Boy and his Dog", the novella later to be made into a film of the same name and also enlarged into the novel, "Blood's A Rover".

July 1974. From the Diamond Dogs Review, performing "Suffragette City".

October 1974. The Soul Tour.

September/October 1974. The Soul Tour, introducing the "Young American".

the success of *Fame*. Bowie was to strike back at RCA the following January when *Low* was released. It was a deliberately non-commercial record inspired by his new surroundings.

David had bought a house in Basle in Switzerland for Angie and Zowie, but he chose to live in a flat above a motor parts shop in Neukoln, a rundown section of Berlin populated largely by Turks, where he could roam the streets totally unrecognized. With his old friend Iggy Pop as a companion, he soaked up the cultural life of Berlin, not only at museums and art galleries but at fuck-clubs and bars. He also allied himself with an elite group of artists, of whom Brian Eno was a member, whose music transcended rock though it was still loosely classified as such. Eno made art for appreciation by intellectuals, not for the masses. Commercial success was a heinous crime.

"I knew I had to get to an environment which was

July 1975, New Mexico. On the set of "The Man Who Fell to Earth".

totally different to LA, so I thought of the most arduous city I could and it was West Berlin," David said at the time of his move. "I needed to lock all my characters away and catch up on living as one solid personality."

Much to Bowie's surprise — and probably annoyance — a single from *Low, Sound and Vision*, was a hit in England. David was outspoken about his apparently sincere wish for the album to flop commercially, adding that he hoped RCA would then release him from his contract thus allowing him

to concentrate on things other than music. He made no attempt to promote *Low* and, instead, appeared as a sidesman with Iggy Pop, touring both Britain and the USA. In the intervening months between the recording of *Low* and it's release, David had produced Iggy's *The Idiot* album. Since David had co-written all the songs and contributed both guitar and saxophone, he was anxious for Iggy's comeback attempt to succeed. He was equally anxious not to steal the show either — and confined himself to keyboards, Iggy's music and no vocal spots.

The Iggy/Bowie tour was notable for one other feature: David overcame his fear of flying. Since the US and UK tours had been booked without taking a lengthy sea voyage into consideration, David relented and flew the Atlantic for the first itme in six years. Since eschewing aerophobia David has traveled extensively by plane to Japan and Africa on private trips, making up for lost time in the past.

The second Berlin album *Heroes*, was recorded, like *Low*, at the Hansa Studios

Circa 1975. Back-stage with Rod Stewart at a Stewart concert.

1970s. The Berlin Wall, pictured here with appropriate graffiti. The Wall is the inspiration for Bowie's song ''Heroes'', and for much of his work to come.

Summer 1975. Film still from "The Man Who Fell to Earth".

which overlook the Berlin Wall. The title track was a song about two lovers meeting by the wall, and the atmosphere of the German city was obviously still David's main influence. Although *Heroes* was more accessible than it's predecessor, it was still a sombre effort which was again aimed at an intellectual audience. Robert Fripp, the eclectic guitarist who made his name with King Crimson, joined Eno as a major contributor alongside the nucleus of David's band: Carlos Alomar (guitar), George Murray (bass) and Dennis Davis (drums). The title track of *Heroes* — one of the strongest songs David had ever written — became another hit single, proving again that David's fans were a loyal bunch regardless of his musical output.

"I felt I was getting predictable and that was starting to bore me," David told writer Michael Watts shortly after *Heroes* was released. "I was entering an era of middle of the road popularity with that soul/disco phase which I didn't like, and it was all getting too successful in the wrong ways. I want and need creative success. I don't

Opposite Page:
Summer 1975. Film still from "The Man Who Fell to Earth".

David Bowie: A Profile 61

want, need or strive for numbers. I want quality, not a rock-and-roll career.

"It doesn't bother me that *Low* and *Heroes* haven't sold as well as my other records. It's rather pleasing in a perverse kind of way. There comes a time when you go through the most ridiculous posture by saying 'I'd be really pleased if everybody stopped buying my records so I could go away and do something else'. At this stage in my life I do feel incredibly divorced from rock, and it's a genuine striving to be that way. I refuse to listen to records these days."

With the release of *Heroes* in October 1977, Bowie elected to actively promote the record for a change, mainly to emphasize his belief in the new music he was creating. He showed up on Marc Bolan's TV Special singing *Heroes* in September, but no sooner had he returned to Berlin than he heard that Bolan had been killed in a car crash. Bowie returned to London to attend his old friend's funeral and stayed at the Dorchester Hotel for a few days to give interviews before flying off to America for a TV appearance with American crooner Bing

Summer 1975. Film stills from "The Man Who Fell to Earth".

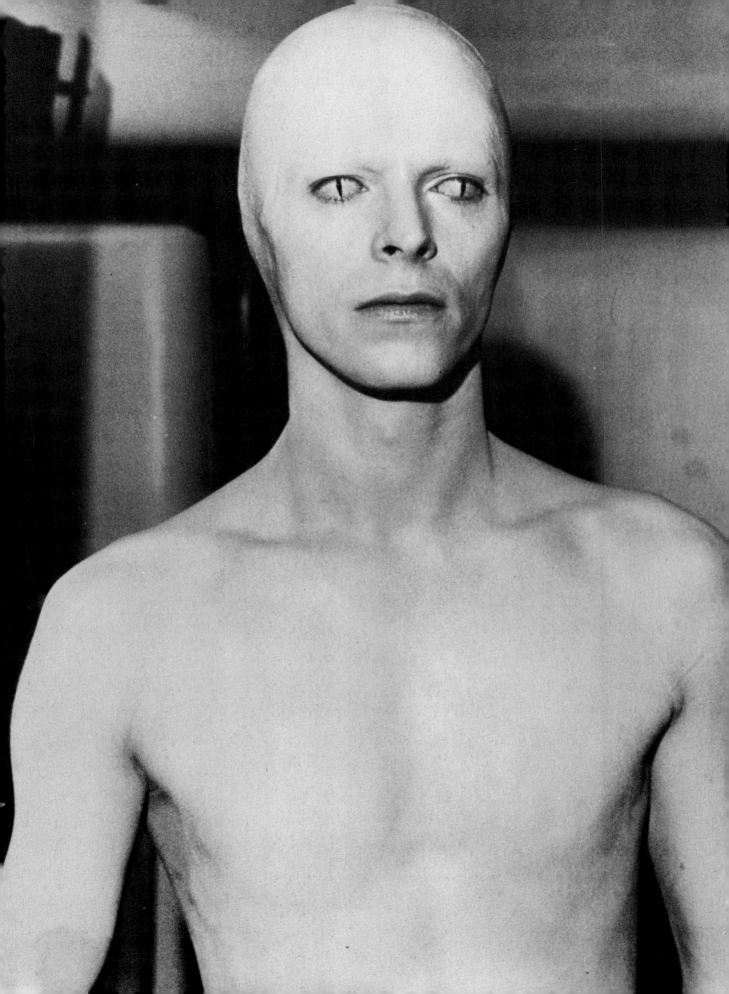

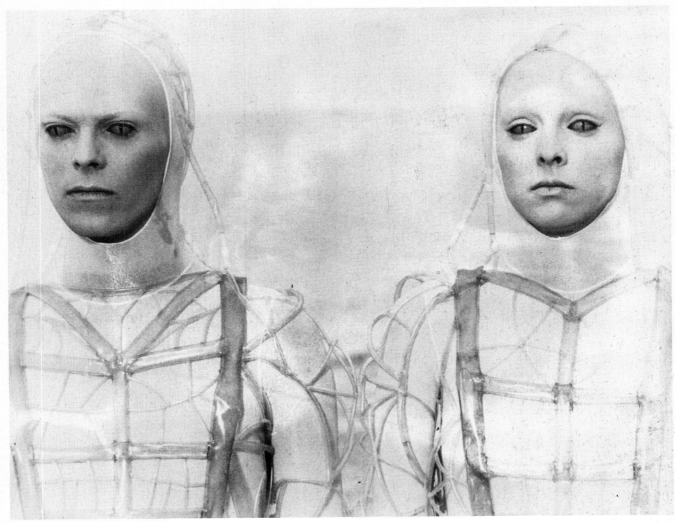

Summer 1975. Film stills from "The Man Who Fell to Earth".

Crosby. By a macabre coincidence Bing Crosby died before the show — a Christmas Special — was aired, and the broadcast was brought forward to November. In it David duetted with the voice of post-war America on a medley of Christmas songs including Rolf Harris' *Little Drummer Boy*.

In December, David returned to Los Angeles to narrate the script for an RCA recording of Prokofiev's *Peter And The Wolf*, which he dedicated to his son Zowie, before setting off on private visits to Japan and Kenya. The beginning of 1978 saw David at work on his second motion picture *Just A Gigolo*, directed by David Hemmings.

Gigolo was shot in Berlin but although the cast included Marlene Dietrich, Kim Novak, Maria Schell, and Curt Jurgens as well as Bowie and Hemmings, it was a commercial failure that David has since disowned. "*Just A Gigolo* is all my 32 Elvis Presley movies rolled into one," he said later. "The film was a cack, a real cack. Everybody who was involved in that film.... when they meet each other now, they look away. I should have known better."

At the end of March David returned to the stage with another spectacular road show that incorporated material from *Low* and *Heroes* with a retrospective journey through his past. He reached back as far as *Ziggy Stardust* for a medley of songs from his

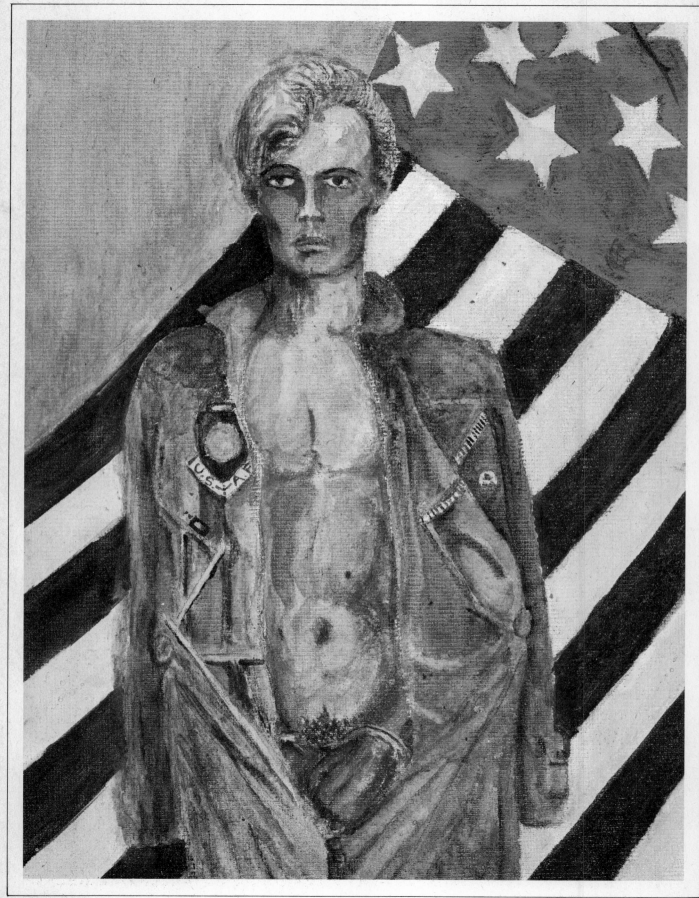

David Dalton
JAMES DEAN
THE MUTANT KING

breakthrough album, and capacity audiences around the world lapped up the program. The American leg of the tour opened on March 29 in San Diego and closed 24 cities later in New York on May 8. After a week's break the tour re-opened in Frankfurt, visiting 19 Continental and British cities before closing in London with three performances at the Earls Court Exhibition Hall, the same venue where the disastrous Ziggy show had almost ended in a riot five years earlier.

David's band on this outing comprised Carlos Alomar, by this time as important a musical ally as David had ever had, and Adrian Belew on guitars, Dennis Davis on drums, Simon House on violin, Roger Powell and Sean Mayes on keyboards and George Murray on bass, and once again there was a spectacular neon white light display designed by Eric Barrett. Several dates

Film still from "The Man Who Fell to Earth".

Circa 1975/76. "James Dean epitomized the very thing that is so campily respectable today — the male hustler. It was part of his incredible magnetism. You know, that he was…a whore. He used to stand on Times Square to earn money so he could go to Lee Strasberg and learn how to be Marlon Brando. He had quite a sordid little reputation. I admire him immensely." Interview, Cameron Crowe, Playboy Vol 23 No. 9.

Late 1975, Los Angeles. David "Rockefeller" Bowie at a business meeting.

Opposite Page:
"The Young American Dream", a painting by Tom Sheridan.

June/July 1975. With Candy Clark. Film still from "The Man Who Fell to Earth".

I think I saw you in an ice-cream
  parlor
drinking milk shakes cold
  and long
Smiling and waving and looking so
  fine, don't think you knew you
  were in this song

David Bowie: A Profile 67

1976 World Tour. London, Wembley Empire Pool.

were recorded and in October RCA released *Stage*, a double live album pressed on yellow vinyl which had been intended as a soundtrack of a tour film. It was the only Bowie album of 1978, and it's release was held up while RCA and David argued over whether it counted as one or two records towards his contracted quota. When it was finally released Bowie took the tour to Australia and Japan where his concerts were greeted with mass hysteria among the nations' youth.

David returned to Europe in December 1978 and spent some time recording his next album, *Lodger*, at the Mountain Studios in Montreux, Switzerland. In the New Year he began promoting *Just A Gigolo* which opened to such poor reviews in Germany that it was taken off the circuit to be re-edited. When the film opened in London on February 14, David turned up for the occasion with a full beard, and met Princess

The Return of the Thin White Duke

An autobiography by David Bowie

Vince was American and came to England, then went to France and became a star of dirge.

But then he came back to England and we spoke of our Findings. He wore a white robe and sandals and we sat in the busy London street with a map of the world and tried to find the people who were passing by and scowling at us. They were nowhere on the map.

Vince went back to France, then I heard about the famous show where he had told his band to go home and appeared in front of the curtains in that old white robe and sandals telling the French people about the comings and goings due upon us. He was banned from performing.

My records were selling and I was being a man in demand. I thought of Vince and wrote "Ziggy Stardust." I thought of my brother and wrote "Five Years." Then my friend came to mind, standing the way we stood in Bewlay Bros. and I wrote "Moonage Daydream."

Excerpt from Bowie's planned autobiography, Rolling Stone, February 1976.

Margaret at the charity premiere. Nevertheless the film bombed and has never been on general release in the UK.

Lodger, a patchy album which saw the return of David's narrative writing style, was released in May, as was a new single *Boys Keep Swinging*, a minor hit. Although *Lodger* was said to contain the best of 22 tracks recorded with Eno, it was not a success, either commercially or artistically, by David's standards. To coincide with its release David visited London briefly for a Capitol Radio broadcast where he joined a dozen fans for a discussion hosted by DJ Nicky Horne. He also appeared on Top of the Pops in a hilarious video of *Boys Keep Swinging* in which he wore three different women's outfits between verses, but he declined all press interviews. Having come to the conclusion that he had made himself too available recently he clammed up and went into hiding for almost 12 months.

In the summer of 1979 the author joined RCA Records at their Bedford

Circa 1976.

Opposite Page:
1976 World Tour. The Thin White Duke onstage.

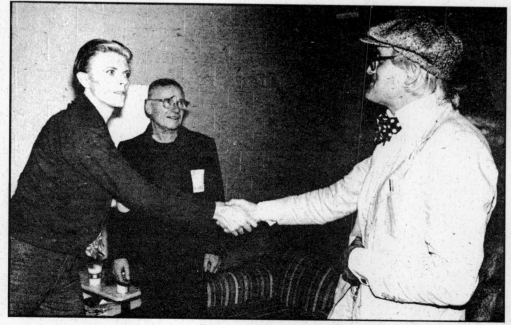
1976. David Bowie meets Christopher Isherwood and David Hockney (right) in Los Angeles.

April 1976, World Tour. With transvestite in Paris night club after the Paris concert.

Avenue offices in London as Senior Press Officer, a position that entailed handling all British press inquiries relating to David Bowie. It soon became apparent that Bowie guards his privacy not only from the press and public but also from his record company. Requests for interviews reached RCA at the rate of several per week, but all were turned down while the whereabouts of David were a closely guarded secret from all but Tony

McGrogan, then the artist liaison manager at RCA. Whenever David came to London he was given the red carpet treatment by RCA, with McGrogan providing the kind of hospitality usually reserved for foreign royalty. This security broke down in April when David was involved in a fracas with Lou Reed at the Chelsea Rendezvous Restaurant in Sydney Street. With reporters present to witness the scene, David and Lou came to blows after a

heated exchange of opinions.

Liaison with David was maintained through his full time PR Barbara De Witt whose offices are in Los Angeles, a location that caused inevitable difficulties in communications with London. Photographs of David were in short supply and he was particularly choosy about which shots should be released to the press. The correct image had to be maintained at all times, and the circulation

of old or non-approved photographs was strictly forbidden.

David came out of his shell at Christmas, 1979, for a brief appearance on Kenny Everett's New Year's Eve Video Show, performing an odd version of *Space Oddity* with acoustic guitar accompaniment in a padded cell. Singles from *Lodger* were released to growing indifference, along with a few miscellaneous odds and ends like the disco version

1976. With Angie.

of *John I'm Only Dancing*
and a desultory version of
Brecht-Weill's *Alabama
Song* which was backed by
the acoustic *Space Oddity*.
Meanwhile David had
obtained a divorce from
Angie, who had returned
to America and was living
in Los Angeles. She was
awarded a lump sum of
$50,000 and David was
given custody of Zowie,
now at a private school in
Switzerland. David
himself was soaking up
Japanese culture in Kyoto
where he had rented a

May 1976. Arriving in England from France, just seconds before giving his famous wave.

July 1977. With Iggy Pop in New York's Ocean Club.

house and interested himself in all things Japanese.

It was a period when the press office at RCA was constantly fending off inquiries about whether David was to leave the label and sign with Warner Brothers, another American conglomerate with a far better track record than RCA as far as record sales were concerned. The truth of the matter was that he owed RCA one more album, which turned out to be *Scary Monsters...And Super Creeps*, released in August, 1980, and coinciding with a dramatic return to public life in all

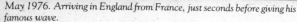

May 1976. Victoria train station, London. "The photographer caught me in mid-wave. I was not giving a Nazi salute," David Bowie says shortly after this notorious incident.

senses of the word.

Just before the album was released David, accompanied as always by personal assistant Corinne Schwab, visited London to meet with RCA executives to co-ordinate the relaese of the album and it's accompanying single *Ashes To Ashes*. Bowie's affinity with RCA in England has always been better than with the parent company in New York where he has been looked upon as a 'safe-bet' for record sales without need of too much promotion. It seems likely that in the near future David will sign with another record company in America while remaining with RCA in Europe.

There are several reasons for this course of action. Should David leave RCA entirely he would lose control of his catalog (16 albums including the two live double sets) and subsequently forfeit all rights to control its marketing, promotion and packaging. He would also lose the opportunity to negotiate an increased royalty rate for these albums, a well known ploy of successful artists who re-sign with the same record company after several years and several albums. Likewise, he would lose the 'star' status he enjoys at RCA, and the enviable

Circa 1976/77. With Iggy Pop on a private visit to Moscow.

March 1977. Playing keyboards on Iggy Pop's March tour.

September 1977. At the funeral of Marc Bolan.

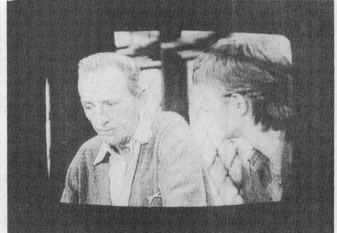

Christmas 1977. With Bing Crosby on American TV. Bing dies a month prior to broadcast.

perks that go with being the company's number one artist. At Warner Brothers, or CBS, or most other large companies, he would become one of a number of star attractions and couldn't expect to receive such lavish treatment from their artist liaison departments. Lastly, of course, it would be a severe blow to RCA's faltering prestige to lose David Bowie — a factor that would certainly influence the company to be more than generous with whatever inducements they offer to retain his services.

At the time of going to press none of these issues had been resolved, and in the summer of 1980 David was still loath to be interviewed by the press, even to promote *Scary Monsters*, by far his most commercial album in three years. In the end he agreed to do interviews with the *New Musical Express* and the *Sunday Times* in England, and both these confrontations took place in Chicago last August.

The previous month Pat Gibbons, David's 'manager', announced that David would be appearing in his first legitimate stage play as John Merrick, the Elephant Man. The

*September 1977, Manchester U.K.
With Marc Bolan at Granada
Television's studios to record Marc's
TV Special — not long before Bolan's
fatal car crash.*

announcement came as no
surprise to the author who
had been forewarned that
"something unusual was
about to happen" but it was
greeted with some cynicism
by certain sections of the
press who believed that the
role had been offered
merely to boost the
box-office. As it turned out

October 1977. Marc Bolan's funeral brings Bowie to England and London's Dorchester Hotel, where he takes a suite to do press interviews for the Heroes album.

January/February, 1978. Publicity still from "Just a Gigolo".

David shot down the cynics with a masterly piece of acting that drew rave reviews from dozens of serious theater critics.

David was offered the role in late 1979 by director Jack Hofsiss who had been impressed with David's work in *The Man Who Fell To Earth*. David jumped at the chance, and joined the Elephant Man company for two weeks of rehearsal in San Francisco before making his debut at the end of July last year in a week long stint at Denver, Colorado. Local theater critics were enthusiastic about his performance and the engagement quickly sold out.

In August the play moved to Chicago's Blackstone Theater for one month, and critics in the Windy City were equally enthusiastic. The play opened in New York at the Booth Theater on Broadway on September 28, and once again the production was a huge success. Reviewing David's performance in the *New York Times*, John Corry wrote: "When it was announced that David Bowie would play the title role in The Elephant Man it was not unnatural to think he had been cast

Opposite Page:
At Granada TV Studios, Manchester, U.K., recording "Heroes" for Marc Bolan's TV Special.

simply for the use of his name. Dismiss that thought now. Yes, more young people in designer jeans and leather now show up at the Booth Theater than before and, yes, they probably show up because Mr Bowie is a celebrated rock star. Fortunately he is a good deal more than that, and as John Merrick, the Elephant Man, he is splendid."

In Chicago, where the author was fortunate enough to see the play on three consecutive nights, David's entrance drew an audible gasp from the audience at each performance. Dressed only in a small loincloth, David first appeared from behind a screen while a sympathetic Dr Frederick Treves gave a graphic account of his appalling disfigurements. While this medical analysis progressed, David contorts himself into the ungainly postures that John Merrick was obliged to live with until his death at the age of 27. The result was a hideously deformed man whose cheerful personality soon won the affection of not only Treves and Victorian Society, but also the theater audience.

It was a gruelling

1978. Publicity of Cherry Vanilla, P.R. lady for Mainman (the company formed by Tony De Fries to manage Bowie).

With Bryan Ferry (centre), leader of Roxy Music, whose arrival on the rock scene in 1973 owed much to Bowie's glamor influence, and John Cale (extreme right), founder-member of Velvet Underground and now a cult rock star in his own right.

schedule for David, even compared to his rock tours. There were eight shows a week including two afternoon performances, and his physical control in maintaining the illusion of Merrick's deformity was quite remarkable. David was obliged to visit a chiropractor almost every day and do exercises before and after each performance to avoid any permanent injury. It took him fifteen minutes to gradually straighten out after each show — any sudden movement might have shattered his spine.

"Over the last three and a half years I've been getting happier and happier," David told *Rolling Stone* reporter Kurt Loder, who was granted an interview backstage while the play was running in Chicago. "Not with myself and my situation, but happier in my realization that I can face up to things a lot better than I could when I was living a heavily rock-and-roll life in America.

"I feel that I can travel about in some kind of anonymity and circulate

Opposite Page:
February 1978. Publicity still from "Just a Gigolo".

Illustration of David Bowie and Lou Reed by Peter Till for Melody Maker, April 1979.

Late 1970s. At keyboards.

within cities I've always dreamed of going to see. More and more I'm prepared to relinquish sales, as far as records go, by sticking to my guns about the kind of music I really want to make. And I'm trying to stretch out, not just to be in there with music but trying to get involved in other avenues

I once used to feel were part of being a quasi-Renaissance man.

"I'm happy that I'm going the way I considered I would be going when I was eighteen years old, which is holding on to nothing and no-one — continually in flux."

David may have been prepared to relinquish

sales, but the fans had other ideas. *Ashes To Ashes* became David's second number one hit in England last August, and *Scary Monsters* followed it to the top of the album charts. A new generation of record buyers were catching up on David's music and the fans who remained from the days of Ziggy Stardust

stayed loyal. While David adopted the Merrick stoop on Broadway, a new movement within the British rock scene, who called themselves The New Romantics, took their inspiration directly from Bowie's style of music and dress.

The New Romantics were not the first British

rock performers from the post punk era whose roots lay in Bowie's work. Gary Numan, a young song writer from Hounslow, enjoyed large record sales throughout 1979 and 1980 with simplified, commercialized variations of Bowie's (and Eno's) synthesized studies that appeared on *Low* and *Heroes*. Utilizing similar staging to Bowie's 'white-light' effects, Numan took to the road with equal success, but his style was too derivative for the critics to take seriously, and he was roundly panned despite his commercial success.

The Romantics — Steve Strange, Spandau Ballet, Adam and the Ants, Ultravox and others — were less obvious than Numan, but their identification with Bowie (and early Roxy Music) was a compliment to his far-sightedness, and further proof of Bowie's qualities as a catalyst for all types of music.

The success of *Scary Monsters* and the link with the New Romantics were factors that led directly to the release of *David Bowie, The Best Of...* on K-Tel Records in January of this year. K-Tel is a company which specializes in leasing tracks from major labels and compiling retrospective albums that are heavily advertised on television. The release of this record,

February 1979. Bowie attends the London premiere of "Just a Gigolo" with actress Sydne Rome who co-stars in the film.

A gift of cosmetics from Charles of the Ritz prompts Bowie to send in return a print of his lips — made with lipstick on a card. The idea is formed to auction the lip prints of other celebrities, in aid of the Save the Children Fund (1979 being the Year of the Child). A charity book of these and other famous lip prints, "With Love From...", which includes this passionate smacker by Bowie, appears in 1980 from George Weidenfeld and Nicolson.

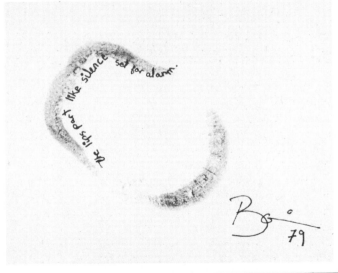

which was a vast improvement on *Changesonebowie*, was timed perfectly, and it rapidly ascended the album charts.

All of which brings the story of Bowie's career up to date. David is now 34 years of age and the father of a nine year old son with whom he spends as much time as possible, whether it be in Switzerland or in America. At the time of writing David is considering taking to the road again in the autumn, and also talking seriously about releasing his art work for public consumption in the form of prints or an exhibition. His presence as an artist, as a rock star or an actor, is as potent today as it was eight years ago when Ziggy Stardust crashed into the public consciousness.

Longevity is a trait all too rare in today's music scene, yet it remains the only true indication of genuine talent. Through change and experiment, David Bowie has survived the fickleness inherent in today's pop culture and emerged as an important, all-round talent with a canny knack of staying a few paces ahead of his rivals. Shrewd yet unpredictable, David Bowie, on current form, is one of the few rock stars whose career as a musician will see him into the nineties, and possibly into the next millenium.

DAVID BOWIE
The Wembley Wizard Touches The Dial

SIDE 1

Station to Station
Suffragette City
Fame
Word on a Wing
Waiting for the Man

SIDE 2

Queen Bitch
Life on Mars
Band Introduction
Changes
TVC 15
Diamond Dogs

HALLOWIEN JACK RECORDS

STEREO

RECORDED LIVE AT WEMBLEY STADIUM LONDON, ENGLAND. 7/5/76

BOWIE
AND THE SPIDERS FROM MARS' LAST STAND
HIS MASTER'S VOICE

THE FIRST FAREWELL TOUR 1973

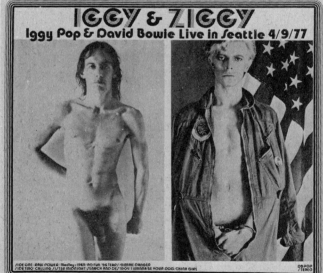

IGGY & ZIGGY
Iggy Pop & David Bowie Live in Seattle 4/9/77

DB/POP
STEREO

POP PIRATES SCUPPERED

By MIRROR CORRESPONDENT

A FIVE-MONTH undercover operation codenamed "Moonbeam" has smashed a pirate record ring.

And pop superstars including Bob Dylan, David Bowie, The Who and Led Zeppelin have won a major battle against bootleggers who cheat the disc industry of £20 million a year.

The victory was claimed minutes after a High Court judge in London accepted undertakings by a number of alleged bootleggers—said to be Britain's biggest syndicate.

They agreed to cease their alleged activities immediately pending a full trial of claims brought against them by British Phonographic Industry Ltd., which has been backed by the major record producers.

BPI obtained court orders a week ago which enabled them to carry out a series of lightning raids in Manchester, Newcastle-upon-Tyne, St. Helens and London on Monday.

Climax

A spokesman said: "Investigators seized equipment and bootleg albums by top artists including David Bowie and Bob Dylan."

The raids were the climax of investigations costing tens of thousands of pounds.

"It will drastically cut the flow of bootleg records and tapes into and around this country," the spokesman added.

Bootleg albums are made at live concerts and then sold to the public with the artists and their record companies getting

Court bid to stop bootleg millions

nothing. A team of BPI investigators used radio cars, long-range cameras and infiltrated the syndicate.

One investigator posed as a manufacturer of bootleg records, even arranging for the pressing of 2,000 Bowie albums from a live Wembley concert.

According to the spokesman, the syndicate also imported American-made discs and distributed them throughout the UK.

Bowie . . . better off

The Who's Roger Daltrey

July 1979. The British Phonographic Institution's controversial tactics in obtaining convictions against bootleg dealers often involves the use of David Bowie's name, and in cases like "Operation Moonbeam" they collude in the alleged manufacture and distribution of the 'illegal' Bowie album, "David Bowie: The Wembley Wizard Touches the Dial", later used in evidence before the High Court in London.

August 1979. At Capitol Radio's London Studios Bowie meets fans, and takes the opportunity to promote the "Lodger" album.

February 1980. "Spent some nights in old Kyoto / Sleeping on the matted ground". Rare shots on holiday in Kyoto, Japan.

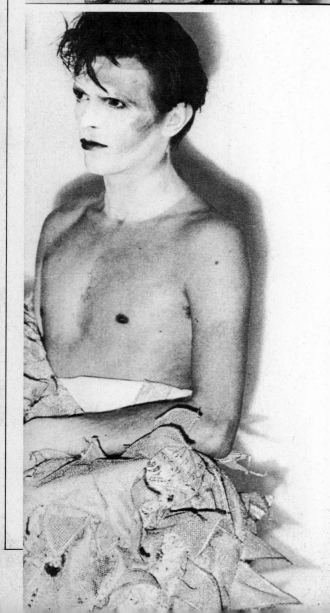

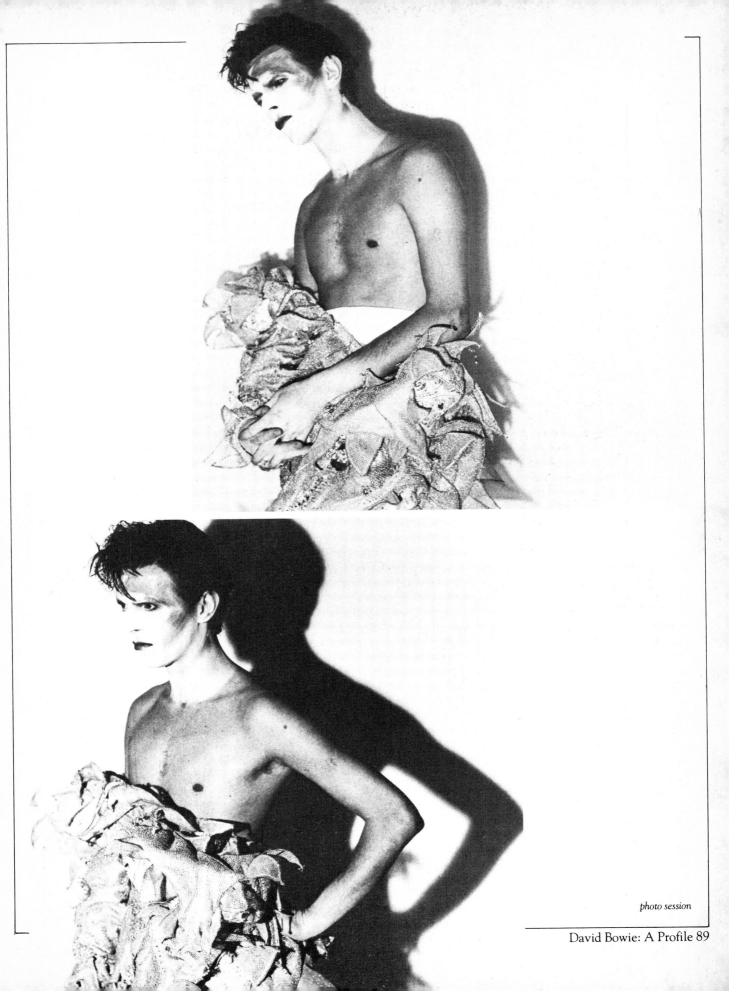

"When I was 14 sex suddenly became all-important to me. It didn't really matter who or what it was with, as long as it was a sexual experience. So it was some very pretty boy in class in some school or other that I took home and neatly fucked on my bed upstairs. And that was it. My first thought was, Well, if I ever get sent to prison, I'll know how to keep happy." "I've always been very chauvinistic, even in my boy-obsessed days. But I was always a gentleman. I always treated my boys like real ladies. Always escorted them properly and, in fact, I suppose if I were a lot older — like 40 or 50 — I'd be a wonderful sugar daddy to some little queen down in Kensington. I'd have a houseboy named Richard to order around." Interview, Cameron Crowe, Playboy, Vol 23 No. 9.

photo session

Circa 1980/81. With Oona Chaplin, widow of Charlie, in New York. Romantic rumors have been denied but the two live close together near Basle, Switzerland.

February 25, 1981, the New London Theatre. Bowie receives Best Male Singer Award in the 1980 Rock and Pop Awards sponsored by the Daily Mirror and the BBC. All winners are voted for by the buying public.

DAVID BOWIE UNOFFICIAL ALBUMS

DISCOGRAPHY
Compiled by Thomas Sheridan

ALBUMS

Ziggy 1 (TUNE IN 001)

Ziggy Stardust
Waiting for the Man
Supermen
Queen Bitch
Suffragette City
White Light, White Heat
Hang on to Yourself — 1
Hang on to Yourself — 2
Moonage Daydream
Watch That Man

All tracks recorded from the BBC Radio program, *Sounds of the Seventies,* May 1972, except *Hang on to Yourself — 2, Moonage Daydream,* and *Watch That Man,* which were recorded at Long Beach Arena, March 10, 1973. Mono.

Ziggy 2 (TUNE IN 002)

Queen Bitch
Bombers
Supermen
Looking for a Friend
Almost Grown
Song for Bob Dylan
Andy Warhol
It Ain't Easy
Bolan Jam

All tracks recorded from the BBC Radio program, *Top Gear,* June 1971 with John Peel, except *Bolan Jam* which was taken from the Marc Bolan television show, September 1978, days before Bolan's death. The album is interesting, but poor quality stereo.

Gentlemen Prefer Blondes (Limp Meat, Hard Hits)

Do Anything you Say
I Dig Everything
Can't Help Thinking About Me
I'm Not Losing Sleep
Supermen
Velvet Goldmine
Hang on to Yourself
Man in the Middle
John, I'm Only Dancing
Amsterdam
Around and Around
Rebel Rebel
Panic in Detroit

A collection of studio tracks, singles and 'B' sides. Stereo.

All American Bowie (TRADE MARK)

My Death
Aladdin Sane
Five Years
Width of a Circle
Ziggy Stardust
Changes
Panic in Detroit
Time
Suffragette City

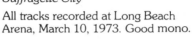

All tracks recorded at Long Beach Arena, March 10, 1973. Good mono.

His Master's Voice (WIZARDO)

Hang on to Yourself
Wild Eyed Boy From Free Cloud / All the Young Dudes / Oh You Pretty Things (medley)
Moonage Daydream
Changes
Space Oddity
Time
Suffragette City
Jean Genie / Love Me Do (medley)
Rock'n'Roll Suicide

All tracks recorded at London's Hammersmith Odeon, July 3, 1973. Bowie's 'farewell' gig. Stereo.

David Bowie at Santa Monica
(KORNYPHONE — Double Album)

Hang on to Yourself
Ziggy Stardust
Changes
Supermen
Life on Mars
Five Years
Space Oddity
Andy Warhol
My Death
Width of a Circle
Queen Bitch
Moonage Daydream
John, I'm Only Dancing
Waiting for the Man
Jean Genie
Suffragette City
Rock'n'Roll Suicide

All recorded for FM Radio, October 20, 1972. Excellent quality, and good patter between tracks by Bowie. Probably the best Ziggy bootleg of all.

Dollars in Drag (The 1980 Floor Show)
(TAKRL)

1984
Sorrow
Everything's Alright
Space Oddity
Supermen
Hang on to Yourself
Man in the Middle
I Can't Explain
Time
Jean Genie
I Got You Babe (with Marianne Faithfull)

All tracks taken from the 'Midnight Special' TV show, October 1973, at London's Marquee Club. Amusing fillers between tracks. Mainly good mono, a few stereo cuts.

Soft in the Middle (TAKRL)

John, I'm Only Dancing
Waiting for the Man
Moonage Daydream
Round and Round
Rebel Rebel
I'm Not Losing Sleep
Can't Help Thinking About Me
Do Anything You Say
I Dig Everything
My Death
Amsterdam

Mainly studio tracks, except for *Waiting for the Man, Moonage Daydream,* and *My Death*, which were recorded live in 1972. Amusing fillers between tracks. Stereo.

The Missing Link (STRAP — Double)

Memory of a Free Festival
Space Oddity
Rebel Rebel
Sorrow
Changes
1984
Moonage Daydream
Rock'n'Roll With Me
Jean Genie / Love Me Do (medley)
Diamond Dogs
Young Americans
It's Gonna be Me
Footstompin'
Can You Hear Me?
Somebody Up There
Suffragette City
Rock'n'Roll Suicide
John, I'm Only Dancing (Again)

Recorded from three different 1974 Soul Tour shows.

Don't Touch That Dial (MARC)

Station to Station
Suffragette City
Fame
Word on a Wing
Stay
Waiting for the Man
Queen Bitch
Life on Mars
Intro
Changes
TVC 15
Diamond Dogs

Japanese bootleg. Recorded in London, May 7, 1976. This record subsequently became *The Wembley Wizard Touches the Dial* when it was allegedly used by the British Phonographic Institution as an 'enticement' in their 'Operation Moonbeam'. Excellent stereo.

Slaughter in the Air
(RUTHLESS RHYMES — Double Album)

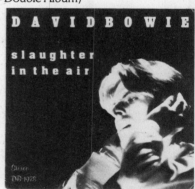

Heroes
What in the World
Be My Wife
Jean Genie
Blackout
Sense of Doubt
Speed of Life
Breaking Glass
Beauty and the Beast
Fame
Five Years
Soul Love
Star
Hang on to Yourself
Ziggy Stardust
Suffragette City
Rock'n'Roll Suicide
Art Decade
Station to Station
Stay
TVC 15
Rebel Rebel
Helden
Heroes (French version)

All tracks live from L.A. Forum, April 4, 1978, except *Helden* and *Heroes* (French version) which are taken from German and French singles respectively.

Wish Upon a Star (WIZARDO)

Waiting for the Man
Word on a Wing
Stay
TVC 15
Panic in Detroit
Fame
Changes
Diamond Dogs

Recorded at the L.A. Forum, February 9, 1976. Stereo.

The Thin White Duke (IMP 1114 — Double Album)

Station to Station
Suffragette City
Fame
Word on a Wing
Stay
Panic in Detroit
Changes
TVC 15
Diamond Dogs
Rebel Rebel
Jean Genie
Can You Hear Me / Young Americans
   (medley duet, with singer Cher)

All tracks live from Nassau Coliseum, March 24, 1976, except medley which is taken from a Cher TV show. Live tracks in stereo.

Stockholm 1979
(RUTHLESS RHYMES — Double Album)

Warszawa
Heroes
What in the World
Be My Wife
Jean Genie
Blackout
Sense of Doubt
Speed of Life
Breaking Glass
Fame
Beauty and the Beast
Intro
Five Years
Soul Love
Star
Hang on to Yourself
Ziggy Stardust
Suffragette City
Art Decade
Alabama Song
Station to Station
Rebel Rebel

Recorded in Stockholm, 1979. Deluxe color cover. Stereo.

SINGLES 45 r.p.m.

Bowie '74 Live (WIZARDO) EP

All the Young Dudes
Cracked Actor
It's Gonna be Me

Recorded early September, 1974, at Universal Amphitheater, Los Angeles. Stereo.

B & B Records Present Bowie & Bing
(B & B)

From the Bing Crosby Christmas Special television show recorded shortly before Bing's death. Available on red, clear, or black vinyl.

ALBUMS (WITH IGGY POP)

Iggy & Ziggy (DB POP STEREO)

Medley 1969
No Fun
96 Tears
Gimme Danger
Sister Midnight
Search and Destroy
I Wanna be Your Dog
China Girl

Recorded live at Seattle, April 9, 1977. Fair to good audience recording.

Stowaway DOA

No Fun
Fun Time
China Girl
Turn Blue
Search and Destroy
I Wanna be Your Dog
TV Eye
Nightclubbing

Recorded live at Santa Monica, April 15, 1977. Good stereo.

Midnight Mantra

A fabulous studio recording of WKZX's studio jam that Bowie and Iggy Pop did at Mantra Studios in Chicago, April 13, 1977.

Suck on This (Double)

Raw Power
TV Eye
Dirt
1969
Turn Blue
Fun Time
Gimme Danger
No Fun
Sister Midnight
I Need Somebody
Search and Destroy
I Wanna be Your Dog
Lust For Life
A Passenger
Nightclubbing
1,2 Brown Eyes

Recorded live at two locations in California and Ohio, April 1977.

I wish to acknowledge David Jeffrey Fletcher's book, *David Robert Jones Bowie: The Discography of a Generalist, 1962-1979,* for some of the listing information for the Iggy Pop/David Bowie and *Missing Link* albums.

AN EVENING WITH
DAVID BOWIE

DAVID BOWIE

THE 1972 AMERCAIN TOUR

Hard Meat And Limp Hits Volume One
BABY
DOLL

Gentlemen still
prefer blondes

STEREO
made in U.S.A.

WRMB 363

SIDE A
Do Anything You Say
I Dig Everything
Can't Help Thinking
   About Me
I'm Not Losing Sleep
Supermen
Velvet Goldmine
Hang On To Yourself

SIDE B
Man In The Middle
John I'm Only Dancing
Amsterdam
Around And Around
Rebel Rebel
Panic In Detroit

DAVID BOWIE